COMPUTER T-SHIRTS

Make T-Shirts
WITH *ANY* COMPUTER PRINTER

Linda Klopp
Bernie Klopp

brainstorm
communications

COMPUTER T-SHIRTS: Make T-Shirts With Any Computer Printer
©Copyright 1995 by Linda Klopp and Bernie Klopp

Library of Congress Cataloging-in-Publication data
Klopp, Linda; Klopp, Bernie - Computer T-Shirts; Make T-Shirts With Any Computer Printer

ISBN 0-9646444-0-1
1. Computer
2. Crafts
3. Graphic Design
4. Desktop Publishing

Library of Congress Catalog Card Number: 95-094376

Printed in the United States of America
Brainstorm Communications
P.O. Box 8570
Baltimore, MD 21234

TABLE OF CONTENTS

Chapter 1

T-Shirts and The New Technology

Designed T-shirts have become a part of our culture. Most of us have adorned ourselves in one at some time or another. In some social circles it is the rare occasion a T is *not* worn! Like the city kid who thinks milk is made in the grocery store, most of us never consider where designed T's come from. The answer, of course, is that they come from the imagination of people like you and me. But the task of getting a T-shirt out of your mind and onto the rack in K-Mart requires a lot of expertise, work and bucks. So we are forced to wear designs from someone else's imagination—the same designs worn by a few thousand other nice people.

A lot us have had T-shirt ideas and even more of us would love to make a design for a retirement roast or a gift for a friend's birthday. But few have actually made the custom shirt because, outside of procrastination, we often lack the know-how or are inhibited by the high cost.

If you have ever bought custom designed T-shirts, you probably had a rude awakening . Each color you want to use requires a separate screen at $15 to $30 each. Each color ink is then added to the cost. Then they tell you about their minimum. They won't print your shirts unless you order two or three dozen. You explain, of course, that there only five bowlers on your team, and you can't justify the price of $150 a shirt. You end up agreeing to buy the shirts for the going price of a tuxedo or you walk away with five very ugly shirts embellished with pressed-on lettering.

THE NEW TECHNOLOGY

Fortunately, all this is changing. Modern technology has made significant inroads into the sometimes mysterious world of custom T-shirts. New materials have been created and old techniques perfected to allow anyone to design their own T-shirt. There are numerous methods to create a unique T-shirt using various types of materials. But without question, the computer generated shirt is the fastest, easiest and most versatile method available. You can now create a high-quality, one-of-a-kind T-shirt right in your own home or office and do it in a matter of minutes using your computer printer with a heat transfer sheet or a special toner cartridge or ribbon.

THE HEAT TRANSFER.

The heat transfer sheet is a specially coated paper that can be printed out of a computer or photocopier and melted into a fabric.

These sheets come in various styles and sizes. The type of computer printer you are using determines the type of transfer sheet needed. Running one of these sheets through your computer printer or photocopier and then heat pressing it onto a T-shirt is all that is needed to create an almost instant T-shirt—and the results are incredible.

The new technology has also created a large number of suppliers. Unlike several years ago, T-shirt materials are now readily available and at competitive prices. For example, well over twenty suppliers now carry heat transfer sheets, while only one company was in this business a few years ago. The Resources section at the end of the manual gives a sampling of suppliers of various materials.

DYE SUBLIMATION TONER CARTRIDGE:

Laser Printer toner cartridges are filled with a dye sublimation toner allowing you to print artwork to ordinary paper and heat press the art onto nearly any fabric or hard surface, such as ceramic and metal.

OTHER METHODS.

But computer generated T-shirts isn't the only area where new technology has made its mark. Advances in other T-shirt design methods have been equally revolutionary. From the new type of glue used in pressed-on letters to the use of new hi-tech screenprinting, T-shirts can now be produced faster and less expensively. These methods can be used when you are trying to get an effect not available from the computer, such as dimensional letters. For an overview of non-computer techniques see Chapter 7, Low Tech T-Shirt Makers.

T's To Draw and Wear!

One method that is not hi-tech but a lot of fun is T's To Draw and Wear. Write, color or paint on this paper, press it on a shirt and you have, in minutes, a custom shirt. Making a T's To Draw and Wear shirt is almost faster than making a phone call! The possibilities for using this technique are unlimited. Kids go wild over this method. The various techniques to use are covered in Chapter 6, *T's To* Draw and Wear.

More Than T-Shirts

The application of these new techniques and materials is not limited to T-shirts. Any fabric is fair game. Kites, doll clothes, (even the doll) and undergarments are a few of the items available for custom designing. Be sure to review the custom ideas outlined in Chapter 8, 101 Things To Make With Computer Transfers.

The mission of *Computer T-Shirts* is to help you take your great ideas and put them on a T-shirt while expending the least amount of effort, time and money, and hopefully, have a lot of fun doing it.

T-SHIRT OCCASIONS:			
Gag Gift	Company Picnic	Mother's day	Teams
Resume	Anniversary	Father's day	Clubs
Birthday	New Baby	Raffle	Organizations
Retirement	Sport Race	Prizes	Events
Reunion	Company logo	Promotions	Thank you
Award	Valentine	Prototype	Best Whatever

Chapter 2

Computer Designing T-Shirts

You can make a customized, one-of-kind T-shirt in minutes by using your computer, a household iron and your imagination!

The computer method of T-shirt design has overcome all the limitations of the older, traditional methods used to customize a T-Shirt. The computer has the potential to print photographs or any design you can imagine, in a rainbow of colors, on only one shirt or thousands, without using special equipment or chemicals. Add to this the low cost and an extremely fast turnaround time and its easy to understand why the computer is fast becoming the custom T-shirt maker of choice. Many traditional T-shirt makers are turning to this process for small orders or shirts requiring multiple colors.

HARDWARE AND SOFTWARE

Of course, the computer equipment and software you have available to you will determine how far you can go in your T-shirt design—you can't, for example, get 256 colors out of a black and white laser printer. But even this limitation can be worked around by using someone else's equipment for output. (more about this later)

Nevertheless, most designs do not require high-end equipment or software. Even the most basic computer software program is capable of producing some really great T-shirt designs when printed out on a dot matrix or black and white laser printer. (black and white could easily be made brown and white, red and white, etc with the change of ribbons or toner cartridge)

More sophisticated programs, particularly drawing programs such as Aldus Freehand, Adobe Illustrator, and Corel Draw, are being used to create designs that only skilled artisans were able to produce using traditional methods.

And, of course, no matter what software you use, the artwork can be stored on disk for future use. While this advantage is obvious, it has a special usefulness for designs that are often updated such as when a new team member needs a shirt with her name.

CUSTOM DESIGN

To custom design only one shirt was unheard of only a few years ago. And getting it printed required days or weeks. But today, with a computer, the only limitation is the imagination.

The days or weeks have been compressed into minutes. Now you can make a unique T-shirt greeting or gift in less time than selecting a greeting card in a store. In the same amount of time you could create original art, make a political or social statement, advertise your services or a special event, wear your club or team logo, or just have fun.

greetings
statements
teams, clubs
events
art

Designing one shirt for yourself or a friend, knowing it is the only one like it in the world, is an exciting proposition. As you get into shirt design, you will soon find hundreds if not thousands of ideas for customizing T's.

One such situation, for example, is designing a shirt with an overall family reunion motif. Individual shirts bear the family member's name—perhaps the person's name could be printed in different colors according to which side of the family they are from. The same technique can be used in other situations where a group needs to be identified as a unit, but with the individual members also identified by name

Any reason or any purpose is an occasion for a custom designed T-Shirt. The T-shirt has become an effective and inexpensive communication medium.

High Quality

The quality of a computer designed T-Shirt is comparable to any other method of T-Shirt design. This technique differs from ironed-on decals which are glued onto the surface of the shirt. The computer generated design becomes a part of the T-shirt. This is because the graphic imprint is *melted* into the fabric. Thus, the imprint lasts as long as the shirt. If applied properly, the image will not fade even with numerous washings.

Since the imprint becomes a part of the fabric, the imprinted area is as flexible and soft as the fabric. The T-shirt industry calls this feature "hand soft"—a term which differentiates the new technology from the 1970 vintage rubberized, stiff imprints or ironed-on transfers that eventually cracked and peeled.

DESIGN T-SHIRT FOR:

Art	Social Statement	Gifts
Decoration	Advertising	Fun
Political Statement	Identity	Shock Value
		Build Team Spirit

THE PROCESS

Making a computer designed T-shirt can be personally reward-ing and a lot of fun. Custom designing really gets those creative juices flowing. And the satisfaction of wearing a design you created only a few minutes earlier is hard to describe.

The whole process is very simple. This is one of those activities that is easier to do than describe. There are three simple steps to getting the custom-designed shirt on your back or into the gift box.

Step 1: *Design* the graphic you will be imprinting on a T-Shirt.

Step 2: *Print* the graphic onto a special Transfer Sheet which you have placed in your printer.

Step 3: *Heat press* the Transfer Sheet onto a T-Shirt.

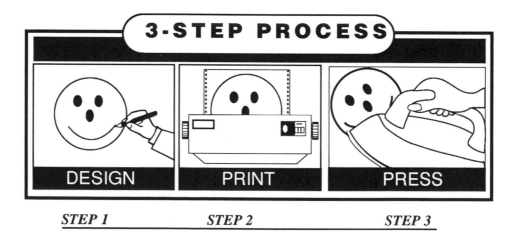

3-STEP PROCESS

DESIGN | PRINT | PRESS

STEP 1　　　　*STEP 2*　　　　*STEP 3*

*One creative use of the copier is to design the graphics on
computer, add color with conventional color tools and then print
the graphic out of a color copier.*

DESIGN: (STEP 1)

Your design can be as simple as a few choice words or as complex as a manipulated photograph. There are simply no limits to what you can design and print on a computer generated T-shirt.

Unfortunately, your computer does lack discernment—it will print a poor design just as easily as it prints a good design. So its up to you to create a good design. A few minutes spent in planning will result in a well-done design that effectively communicates your message. A sure sign of an amateur designer is a T-shirt displaying a hodgepodge of graphic elements that says nothing!

When designing a T-shirt, <u>less is often better than more</u>. Like a poster or billboard, a T-shirt should have one message, and that message has to be grasped in a glance, within three to five seconds. A few simple elements, words or graphics usually does the job best. Remove unnecessary items.

CREATING A DESIGN IDEA:

Here are a few techniques to make your design accomplish its purpose. Actually, that's the first step—defining your purpose. If you are trying to have Aunt Martha blush when she opens your birthday gift, think of things that will make her blush. That's your purpose. Leave the highbrow art and clever sayings to others or another day. The task at hand is to do nothing more than accomplish your purpose—make Aunt Martha blush when she sees your T-Shirt creation.

Take a few seconds to write a brief description of the *purpose*. Jot down a few things that will help you *accomplish* this purpose. For example: The *purpose* is to get Aunt Martha to blush. You know she will blush at anything risque. So to *accomplish* your purpose, you need to make a risque design or statement. Next, start generating ideas.

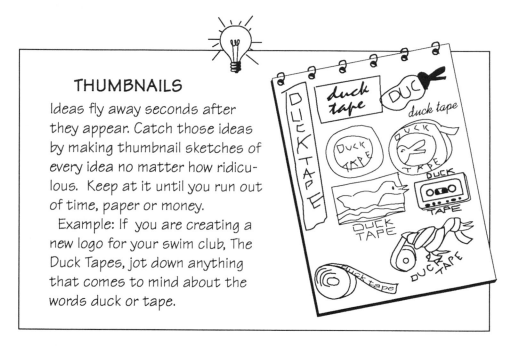

THUMBNAILS

Ideas fly away seconds after they appear. Catch those ideas by making thumbnail sketches of every idea no matter how ridiculous. Keep at it until you run out of time, paper or money.

Example: If you are creating a new logo for your swim club, The Duck Tapes, jot down anything that comes to mind about the words duck or tape.

THE BLANK PAGE SYNDROME:

A lot of people never get beyond this point because of the "blank page syndrome". Don't allow the blank page to inhibit you—just start. Starting something, no matter how trivial or unrelated, is better than not starting. Even if your first efforts amount to no more than doodling or drawing stick figures, ideas will be eventually generated. Starting is 90% of creating a successful design. And remember, a successful design is not necessarily one that wins awards and the accolades of all your peers. Rather, it is a design that accomplishes what *you* want it to accomplish—your purpose. If Aunt Martha blushes, you have created a winner.

When your idea generator seems to be out of power, look

for design ideas in books and magazines. The point here is stimulation, not plagiarism. This exposure to other's design jump starts your idea generator. When you start brainstorming (even if you are alone) you will get ideas, some great, some lousy. Put them all down on paper immediately. You can bet the farm your ideas will flee two seconds after you get them if you haven't recorded them. Continue making rough thumbnail sketches. Keep the thumbnails coming until you get tired, bored or run out of ideas.

The above approach works well for most people, but not all. There are a few who need to process design ideas in their mind and end up with the one design idea they will use. They neither pick up a pencil nor turn on the computer. This type of designer is a rare person and to watch them do this is an awesome experience. Nearly as rare is the person who is able to process their ideas right on the computer screen and reach a final design decision within seconds.

GETTING YOUR DESIGN INTO THE COMPUTER

Place the essential elements (text, graphics, photos) on the computer screen and play with them, trying out each idea from your thumbnail sketches. The design that excites you will rarely resemble your original sketch idea. The design somehow evolves out of the trying out of ideas.

When you develop a design that you like, STOP. If you like it that is all that really matters. You will never ever never ever make a design that absolutely everybody likes. No one can. Print your work as a rough draft to paper if you feel it might need tweaking, but don't allow any self-doubting to reject your design.

The very second you begin wondering if its good enough those little gremlins of doubt will tell you how bad it really is and how people will laugh at you. Don't even let them start— keep busy by getting your computer ready for a final printout. Creativity is a fragile thing, guard it jealously.

ZEROS
straight-up

ZEROS
arch

ZEROS
vertical arch

ZEROS
bridge

ZEROS
arched bridge

ZEROS
connected bridge

ZEROS
pennant

ZEROS
reverse

SPORTS LETTERING STYLES

Computers with drawing programs are capable of creating sports lettering styles. These lettering systems are also available in some clip art collections, or can be scanned in from another source. Finished dimensional lettering is also a feature of the pressed-on lettering format. (See Chapter 7, Low-Tech T-Shirt Maker

ZEROS
double letter

ZEROS
vertical

Zeros script

Zeros script w/Tale

ZEROS Collegiate

ZEROS Block

ZEROS Serif

Zeros

TEAM ZEROS

ZEROS

ENLARGED DINGBAT CAN BE USED LIKE CLIP ART

An often overlooked art source is the dingbat or other type of non-letter font such as ornaments, symbols and woodcuts.

When enlarged, these symbols are effective in communicating an idea, especially when coupled with text typed over, around or under the symbol. Next time you are stuck for a graphic, try dingbats-the forgotten art source!

DINGBATS AS ART!

GEOMETRIC SHAPES HAVE LOTS OF POTENTIAL

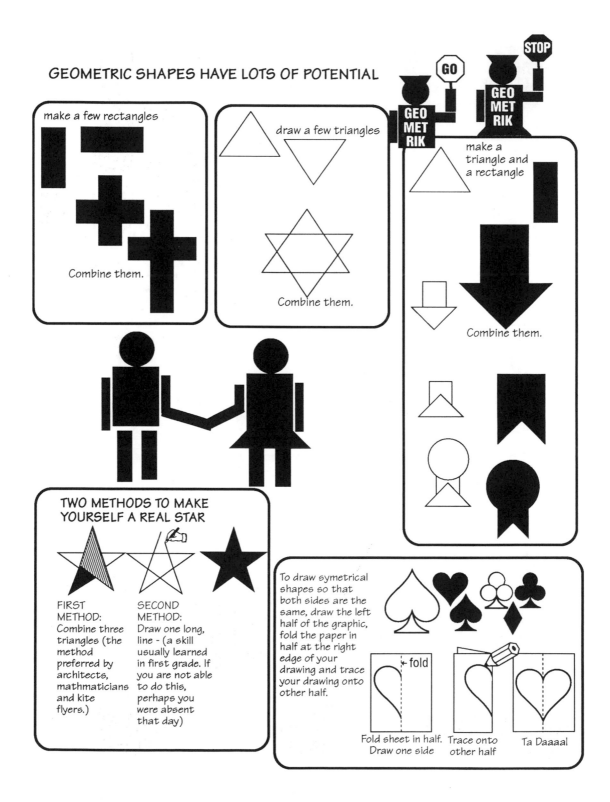

make a few rectangles

Combine them.

draw a few triangles

Combine them.

make a triangle and a rectangle

Combine them.

GEO MET RIK

GO

STOP

GEO MET RIK

TWO METHODS TO MAKE YOURSELF A REAL STAR

FIRST METHOD: Combine three triangles (the method preferred by architects, mathmaticians and kite flyers.)

SECOND METHOD: Draw one long, line - (a skill usually learned in first grade. If you are not able to do this, perhaps you were absent that day)

To draw symetrical shapes so that both sides are the same, draw the left half of the graphic, fold the paper in half at the right edge of your drawing and trace your drawing onto other half.

← fold

Fold sheet in half. Draw one side

Trace onto other half

Ta Daaaal

GREAT GRAPHICS FROM SIMPLE SHAPES

Often, simple drawings can be used to make effective graphics. Great artistic ability isn't necessary to create some really neat stuff—here we have a few ideas for making graphics from circles and geometrics.

These are only a few of the thousands of graphics possible by combining simple shapes. Add a few words and you have a T-shirt design that is uniquely your own.

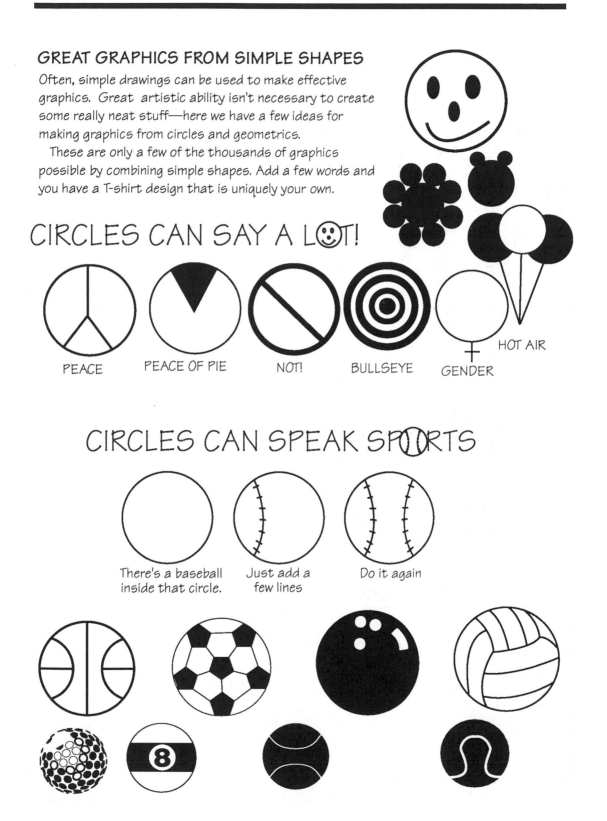

CIRCLES CAN SAY A LOT!

PEACE   PEACE OF PIE   NOT!   BULLSEYE   GENDER   HOT AIR

CIRCLES CAN SPEAK SPORTS

There's a baseball inside that circle.

Just add a few lines

Do it again

USING COMPUTER FONTS WITH IMPACT

Wording on T-shirts is an often used and effective design technique. Any style of lettering will tell the message. However, the impact of the message will be hightened by using a lettering style that speaks the same language.

Peking, for example, says "chinese" more effectively when written in an oriental style type.

A large variety of typefaces are installed on many computers or can be created in a drawing program.

Pressed-on letters is an alternative method of lettering T-shirts with impact.

SOUTHWESTERN
NO NONSENSE
TRADITIONAL
ARCHITECTURAL
R.S.V.P.
Collegiate
DAGGERS AND DRAGONS
Casually Speaking
UPTOWN Theatre
PARCEL POST
THE NEW Old
Handwitten

CREATING A "FEEL" USING COMPUTER MANIPULATION

Contrasts give impact to message. Large and tiny words next to each other, for example, sends an unspoken message and grabs attention. Many computer programs are capable of manipulating type. Try out various approaches, but keep the message simple, easy to understand at a glance.

HEAVY
THIN
SQUEEZE
BIG LITTLE

USING PHOTOGRAPHS

Photographs can be imprinted on T-shirts using the computer to transfer the photo. A photograph must first be brought into the computer by using a digital input device. These digital devices, such as scanners, translate the various shadings of a photograph into numbers (digits) that the computer can read. After the photo is digitized, it can be printed by itself, incorporated into your design, or altered if you have access to a photo manipulation program such as Adobe Photoshop.

If you plan to use photos in your design, refer to Chapter 5 for more detailed information and helpful hints.

COPYRIGHTS

Their Copyrights

Take a few seconds to make certain the graphics you are using are not copyrighted. Graphics can also include words, phrases and sentences. Some copyright holders are vigilant in protecting their exclusive rights to a graphic's usage. And, of course, using someone else's property without their permission is stealing.

If you absolutely have to use the copyrighted item, contact the copyright holder. They will often give you an O.K. (hopefully in writing) if you are printing only one or two T-shirts. Don't forget to put the encircled letter c "©" next to the graphic.

This liberal policy may not necessarily apply to licensed copyright products such as sports teams logos or cartoon characters such as Mickey Mouse®. The copyright holders license their graphics for a fee to companies who sell the graphic im-

---

Contrary to popular belief, the word
copyright *does not mean*
"the right to copy"!

---

printed on various products. Unless you hold a license from the copyright holder, don't even think of copying these graphics!

Several companies carry complete lines of licensed imprinted products. The Bodek and Rhodes Company, *(see resources)* for example, will supply you with any kind of apparel bearing the official logos and colors of national sports teams, such as Yankees®. The encircled R ® is used for a registered trademark. Trademarks require a more expensive application and search process usually done by attorneys.

The Copyright line is written as:

Copyright © Your Name, Year/All rights reserved

Your Copyrights

Protecting your intellectual creation is a simple process. Get a copyright form from the copyright office in Washington, fill it out and return it with the fee, about $10. You now have the exclusive right to reproduce the copyrighted work. Copyrighted work should always be noted as such by placing the copyright symbol adjacent to the graphic.

You'll be surprised how the average person reacts to copyrighted designs. Somehow they think it is more valuable, more "designer" quality than uncopyrighted design!

Copyright Office
Library of Congress
Room 401
Washington, DC 20540

PRINT (STEP 2)

Anything you can normally print on your computer printer can also be printed and transferred onto a T-shirt. This is accomplished by using a special heat transfer sheet in place of the regular paper.

All computer printers can use transfer sheets, but the type of transfer sheet and the method of using them differs between different types of printers. Certain printers can use special toner cartridges or ribbons instead of the special heat transfer sheet.

For printing T-shirts, computer printers can be classified as either Multi-Color Capable or One Color Capable

---

TYPES OF MULTI-COLOR PRINTERS

Dye-Sublimation - A type of full-color printer which melts dye from a ribbon, transferring it onto paper.

Thermal Wax - A type of full-color printer which melts wax from a ribbon, transferring it onto paper.

Ink-Jet (Bubble Jets) - A type of printer which sprays a carefully controlled ink dye onto the surface of paper. Some ink jet printers are capable of full color printing.

Laser Dye-Sub - An ordinary laser printer in which four separate toner cartridges are used to make a full-color print. This method requires four separate passes through the printer.

MULTI-COLOR CAPABLE PRINTERS

If you plan to use lots of colors in your design, you'll need to print on a multi-color printer— a Thermal Wax, Dye-Sublimation or color Ink-Jet (Bubble Jet) printer. These printers have the potential to print every color of the rainbow and then some. Its hard not to be impressed with the quality output of these machines.

If you don't own one of these printers you can copy your artwork to a diskette and have it printed out by a computer service bureau or a company owning a color printer. You may need to supply them with the special heat transfer sheet.

When you send computer files out to be printed be sure to include on your diskette all screen and printer fonts you used plus any graphics such as (.tif) and (.eps) files you may have imported into your artwork. Files larger than the capacity of a diskette may be copied to several diskettes or to a large capacity disk such as Syquest, Optical or DAT. Check with the person who will be outputting your files to determine what type of disk

> **Service Bureaus** are companies in the business of supplying various computer-centered services to the pre-press printing industry. Graphic design, advertising, desktop publishers, and printing firms are the Bureaus typical client. If you can't find the name and number of a Bureau in the yellow pages, call one of the firms using these services and ask them who they use. If the Bureau doesn't have the equipment you need, ask them who does-be diligent, somebody, somewhere has it.

media is acceptable.

Wax Thermal printers

Wax Thermal printers use their regular printer ribbon with a special heat transfer paper. When ordering sheets, specify the size sheet you want and the brand of machine you are using. Heat transfer sheets are available for both the 8 1/2" x 11" and the 11"x17" printer. These transfers are hand ironable but require a practice run to determine the pressure and heat adjustments. Be aware, however, the manufacturer recommends using a commercial heat press. (see Heat Press discussion below)

These printers use a gripper system to pull the paper through the machine. A clamp grips the end of the paper, taking up some of the paper length. This one to one and a half inch "gripper" area reduces the actual graphic print area. For example, an 8 1/2" x 11" sheet has an actual print area of only 8" x 8" inches minus the gripper space.. (To get a full 11 inches, use the 11"x14" transfer if the machine is legal-size capable) If you are using someone else's printer, check with them on what image size is available to print.

Ink Jets (Bubble Jets)

Ink Jets use their standard cartridge with a special heat transfer paper. When ordering transfer sheets, specify the size you will be using.

Several vendors also carry thermal ink jet cartridges. With these, use your regular paper. While these cartidges do an adequate job, the ink jet transfer paper is the method of choice because of their sharper output, their "on the fly" convenience (you don't have to change cartridges), and their lower initial cost. Even though these transfers are hand ironable, the manufacturer believes the best results are achieved with a commercial heat press. (see Heat Press discussion below)

You may have to shop around to find sizes larger than 8 1/2" x 11". Check with the vendors in the Resource section. If they don't carry the larger sizes they will be happy to tell you who does.

Dye-Sublimation

Dye-Sublimation printers use their normal ribbon, but unlike other printers, printing is not done directly onto a heat transfer. The graphic is first printed onto plain paper. This paper is then heat pressed onto a special transfer sheet. This transfer sheet is then pressed onto the garment. With a little practice you can hand iron these transfers; however, the manufacturer believes best results are achieved with a commercial heat press. (see Heat Press discussion below)

When ordering transfer sheets both the sheet size and printer brand must be considered. These sheets are available from several dealers. The quality of the dye-sublimation printed T-shirt graphic is incredible.

Further information on using dye-sublimation printers is given in Chapter 4.

ONE-COLOR
CAPABLE
PRINTERS

Dot Matrix - A type of printer which presses a series of pins through a ribbon, onto paper creating dots. The dots are placed close together in such a way as to create letters and numbers.

Laser - A computer printer using powdered toner which is laid down on paper by a laser emitting light.

ONE-COLOR CAPABLE PRINTERS

Laser Printer

T-shirt designs can be printed with the laser printer by using either of two methods.

Method 1. *A special toner cartridge*, printing to plain paper. This paper is then pressed onto the shirt. The special toner cartridge is used in place of the regular cartridge and can be purchased in several colors. Switching the different color cartridges permits printing a multiple-colored shirt with solid colors (as opposed to process colors like in a photograph) If you plan to print shirts frequently or in large quantities, the toner cartridge method is the way to go. This method produces excellent graphics.

Method 2. *A special heat transfer sheet* using the printer's regular toner cartridge. Simply insert the transfer sheet in the feeder tray as you would with regular paper.

For occasional T-shirt designs, this less expensive transfer sheet is a better choice. You may have to shop for suppliers of larger size sheets such as 11"x17". The standard 8 1/2" x 11" is available from several dealers. Several vendors carry both the sheets and the cartridges.

Special felt tip dye pens and paints can be used to add color to the design if you wish.

Dot Matrix Printers

Designs can be printed using dot matrix printers by either of two methods.

Method 1. *A special ribbon*, printing to plain paper. The special ribbon is inserted in place of the regular ribbon and printing is done on whatever paper you regularly print on. While this method is more time consuming than method 2, transfer ribbons are available to permit printing in several colors. Check resource section for vendors who carry these ribbons. Printers with track feeding may find the ribbon method easier to use than the transfer sheet approach.

Method 2. *A special heat transfer sheet* using the printer's regular ribbon. Simply print onto this sheet and its ready to press onto the shirt! If you are using a black ribbon and don't require a color print out, this is the way to go. This transfer is very easy to use and corrections can be made if necessary right on the transfer. It is far easier to use than Method 1 since ribbons do not have to be switched each time you want to print a T-shirt!

For multi-color ribbons (available on some printer models) the transfer sheet has an even greater potential.

This transfer in the 8 1/2 x 11" size is readily available from several suppliers. For larger than normal sizes, or track fed paper, you may have to shop a few dealers. Start with those listed in the Resource section of this manual.

If desired, color can be added to this heat transfer sheet method by using everyday felt tip pens, crayons or paint . Use the computer to make an outline of the design; you just fill in the outline with color as if you were drawing in a coloring book.

Craft people use this transfer sheet to create designs on fabrics. The lines of the design are used as a guide for cross-stiching or other crafting techniques.

Excellent results can be had by hand ironing these transfers. The manufacturer, however, believes the best results are achieved with a commercial heat press. (see Heat Press discussion below)

PRESS: (STEP 3)

Apprehensive probably best describes how most people approach their first attempt at pressing the heat transfer sheet onto a T-shirt. After the first successful pressing the apprehension goes away and the whole process becomes easy and effortless, without any trepidation whatsoever.

The job is accomplished by placing the transfer sheet on the shirt, pressing the transfer with heat and then removing it. There are a few techniques to make the whole thing work better and easier and a few glitches to avoid. The following section tries to show you the best techniques to use while trying hard not to scare you into thinking this is difficult. It's a lot easier than it seems!

<u>FIRST</u>, Place the paper face down on your T-shirt

Cut away any excess (unprinted) portion of the printed transfer sheet, leaving about 1/4" all around the design. You can get away without doing this if the outline of the whole transfer sheets doesn't bother you.

Take the printed transfer sheet and place it face down (the designed side) on the T-shirt at the position you wish to have it printed. You can make sure it is positioned straight by first folding the designed transfer in half vertically and using the fold as a guide. Putting a fold-crease on the shirt will make things even easier. Then, all you have to do is match the transfer's crease against the shirt's crease. (see illustration on facing page)

This is the technique used in most situations. There are exceptions, though. Printing on a dark shirt requires you to first press a special sheet onto the shirt before positioning your transfer sheet. (see the *Opaquing* section)

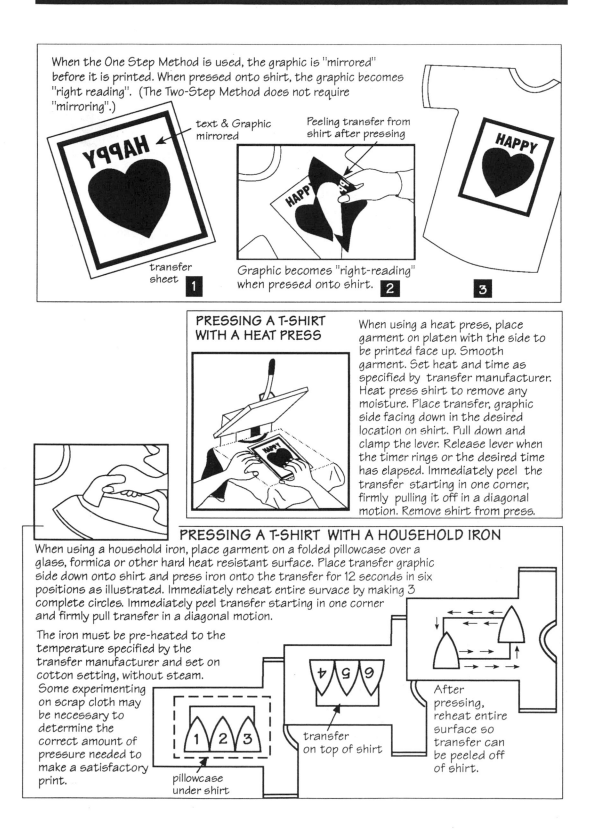

When the One Step Method is used, the graphic is "mirrored" before it is printed. When pressed onto shirt, the graphic becomes "right reading". (The Two-Step Method does not require "mirroring".)

text & Graphic mirrored

Peeling transfer from shirt after pressing

HAPPY

transfer sheet **1**

Graphic becomes "right-reading" when pressed onto shirt. **2**

3

PRESSING A T-SHIRT WITH A HEAT PRESS

When using a heat press, place garment on platen with the side to be printed face up. Smooth garment. Set heat and time as specified by transfer manufacturer. Heat press shirt to remove any moisture. Place transfer, graphic side facing down in the desired location on shirt. Pull down and clamp the lever. Release lever when the timer rings or the desired time has elapsed. Immediately peel the transfer starting in one corner, firmly pulling it off in a diagonal motion. Remove shirt from press.

PRESSING A T-SHIRT WITH A HOUSEHOLD IRON

When using a household iron, place garment on a folded pillowcase over a glass, formica or other hard heat resistant surface. Place transfer graphic side down onto shirt and press iron onto the transfer for 12 seconds in six positions as illustrated. Immediately reheat entire survace by making 3 complete circles. Immediately peel transfer starting in one corner and firmly pull transfer in a diagonal motion.

The iron must be pre-heated to the temperature specified by the transfer manufacturer and set on cotton setting, without steam. Some experimenting on scrap cloth may be necessary to determine the correct amount of pressure needed to make a satisfactory print.

pillowcase under shirt

transfer on top of shirt

After pressing, reheat entire surface so transfer can be peeled off of shirt.

The dye sublimation and a few other process also use this two-step method in which the transfer sheet is first pressed onto another sheet before placing on the shirt. More about this later in the Chapter 4, "Nitty Gritty"

THEN: Heat press the paper into the shirt fabric:

Transferring your design image into the shirt fabric is accomplished by heat and pressure. The amount of pressure and heat to apply is determined by several variables such as: Type of fabric to be pressed, type of transfer sheet being applied, and type of pressing equipment being used.

T-shirt fabric is either 100% cotton or a blend of cotton and a synthetic material such as polyester. (see facing page) All transfer sheets will print onto Cotton blends, a few will work with 100% cotton. Both fabrics require about the same amount of heat and pressure. However, non-cotton fabrics vary dramatically. The specific heat and pressure to use for your situation is covered in the Nitty Gritty chapter.

Heat Transfer manufacturers usually suggest proper heat and pressure settings. Nevertheless, non-cotton fabrics should be test pressed on a scrap piece of cloth before pressing your final design. This needs to be done only on the first job. The settings will apply to everything else you do with that fabric.

Be extremely careful not to move the transfer on the shirt once the transfer or shirt is hot. Moving the transfer will create smears on your shirt which cannot be removed.

An ordinary household iron set to a cotton setting (do not use steam) will work great with just about any transfer. This will probably be the only heat press you will ever need. If, however, you plan to do a large number of shirts or find you need a more sophisticated method, then you will need to look into accessing a Heat Press. (see heat press information below)

Manufacturer of heat transfers may not recommend hand ironing their transfers. They believe the best results are achieved with a commercial heat press. (see Heat Press discussion below)

   T's are available in several weights and fabrics. Some transfer sheets can be printed on 100% cotton, others require a percentage of synthetic content. For example, dye-sublimation needs a percentage of synthetic material. Check the transfers you are using to determine which shirts to buy.

FABRIC:
   100% Cotton
   60/40 (60% cotton, 40% Polyester)
   50/50 (50% cotton, 50% Polyester)

WEIGHT:
   Promotional-The lightest weight T, suitable for giveaways. Close in weight to an undershirt.

   Premium-Middleweight, the most common type sold by T-shirt manufacturers.

   Heavy Weight-Highest quality and price. If you want a good T, this is the one to get.

POPULAR T-SHIRT BRANDS

Print Ons
Screen Stars
Hanes
Fruit of The Loom
Oneita
Screen Gems
Tultex
Lee
Also see
  Resources

THE UNUSUAL

Color Change T-Shirts: This shirt changes color with your moods!
Irregulars: Shirts with manufacturing flaws sold "as is" and at deeply discounted prices
Belt Prints: Shirts are printed over entire outer surface.
Private Label: Your own label is sewn on the shirt in place of the manufacturer's label.

SHIRT SIZES

ADULT:	YOUTH:	TODDLER:	INFANT
Small	2	6 Mo	
Medium	4	12 Mo	
Large	5/6	15 Mo	
Extra Large		24 Mo	
Up to 8XL			

Let The Buyer Beware

Heat transfers can be applied with a household iron, but some, such as opaque and copier transfers, take a bit of skill. The pressure you apply must be consistent over the entire transfer and heat must be kept close to the manufacture's suggested heat setting.

As suggested later in the book, practice on scrap fabric before you do your final pressing.

Many heat transfer manufacturers do not recommend using a household iron to apply **any** of their transfers. They suggest their transfers be applied **only** with a commercial heat press. If you chose this route, see the "Heat Press" section below for sources.

LASTLY: Remove the paper:

After pressing the Heat Transfer Sheet into the shirt fabric, remove it by picking loose a corner and peeling the transfer from fabric using firm, steady pressure. Transfers must be peeled immediately while still hot. If it appears your transfer will not peel off easily and in one piece, reapply heat with a firm pressure being certain that the iron covers all edges and cor-

---

Heat and pressure settings also vary somewhat between Heat Transfer Sheet manufacturers. Follow their directions, but again, do a test run on a scrap of cloth.

---

ners. The transfer should now peel off easily.

HEAT PRESS:

A Heat Press is essentially an iron with a large heat surface. The garment is placed onto the platform (ironing board), the transfer is placed on top of the garment, and the top (iron) is closed down against the platform. This system allows the transfer sheet to be pressed and heated in one step. The heat press has temperature and pressure adjustments.

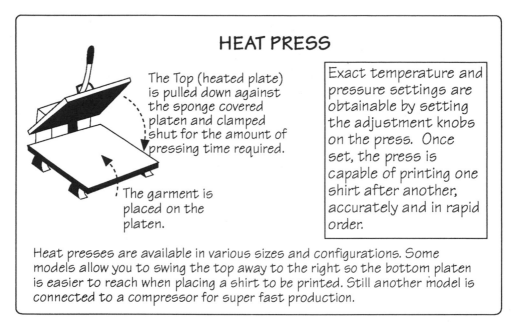

HEAT PRESS

The Top (heated plate) is pulled down against the sponge covered platen and clamped shut for the amount of pressing time required.

Exact temperature and pressure settings are obtainable by setting the adjustment knobs on the press. Once set, the press is capable of printing one shirt after another, accurately and in rapid order.

The garment is placed on the platen.

Heat presses are available in various sizes and configurations. Some models allow you to swing the top away to the right so the bottom platen is easier to reach when placing a shirt to be printed. Still another model is connected to a compressor for super fast production.

A Heat Press sells in the $400 to $1000 neighborhood. Used presses are sometimes listed in classified ads of local newspapers and screenprinting trade journals.

In larger cities presses are available for renting. Or, you might want to farm the work out. There is someone in your area who has a heat press. In a large metropolitan area there may be hundreds.

A small T-shirt shop is the best bet. Most heat press owners will do your pressing for free or a nominal fee. Many dry cleaners have a type of press that will work fine with heat transfers. Just be sure they don't require steam to operate.

A Photo Mounting Press, a piece of equipment used by photographers, can be used in place of a heat press. While you have to do your own timing and other adjustments manually, this equipment is able to do a very good job of T-shirt pressing.

Who Has a Heat Press?

Dry Cleaners
Mall T-shirt retailers
T-Shirt Shops
Screenprinters
Photographers

Call or visit one of these establishments. If they do not have a heat press they will probably know someone who does.
Also see list on page 52.

CARE INSTRUCTIONS

Nearly every heat transfer manufacturer tags a "care" warning onto their product. However, most T-shirt owners use normal laundering methods without any adverse affects.

For the record, here is the typical warning:

1. Turn garment inside out.
2. Do not use bleach.
3. Wash in cool/warm water using mild detergent.
4. Set dryer at "cool" setting, line dry or dry flat.
5. Do not re-iron surface.

OPAQUE PRINTING (PRINTING ON DARK COLORED FABRIC)

Computer generated transfers do not work well with dark fabrics. Because the transfer graphic actually melts into the fabric, the graphic color and the dark fabric color combine to make a muddy colored graphic. The work around for this limitation is the opaque transfer sheet.

When applied, Opaque sheets appear to be glued on top of the fabric rather than melted into the fabric like other transfer methods. Nevertheless, the fabric/transfer graphic is soft and provides a very attractive appearance.

The opaque sheet from Wyndstone (See Resource Section) seems to work better than most. At a glance, it is difficult to tell that their opaqueing material was used to create the graphic.

To print on dark fabrics a two step method is used.

Print your image onto a regular heat transfer sheet.

1. Place a special opaque sheet on the platen of your heat press, with the smooth side down. Put the printed heat transfer sheet image side down, on top of the white side of the opaquing and press for 2-4 seconds at 375 degrees Fahrenheit. (This bonds the image to the opaquing.)

Trim this sandwiched pieces on a flat cutting surface. Use an Exacto® knife, a fabric cutting wheel (sold in fabric or notions stores) or any other precision cutting tool along with a metal edge ruler.

The entire graphic should ideally fit into a geometric shape as trimming irregular shapes is tedious if not impossible. If your graphic has an irregular shape, fill in the surrounding area with solid, patterned of designed element—that is, fill in the non-graphic area to create a geometric shape.

Separate the smooth liner from the opaquing material.

2. Position image on garment, with the white side down. Heat press, using 375 degrees Fahrenheit, for 20-30 seconds, with heavy pressure. Allow to cool for 5 seconds before peeling. (Only the Heat Transfer sheet is peeled)

Placement Of Transfers

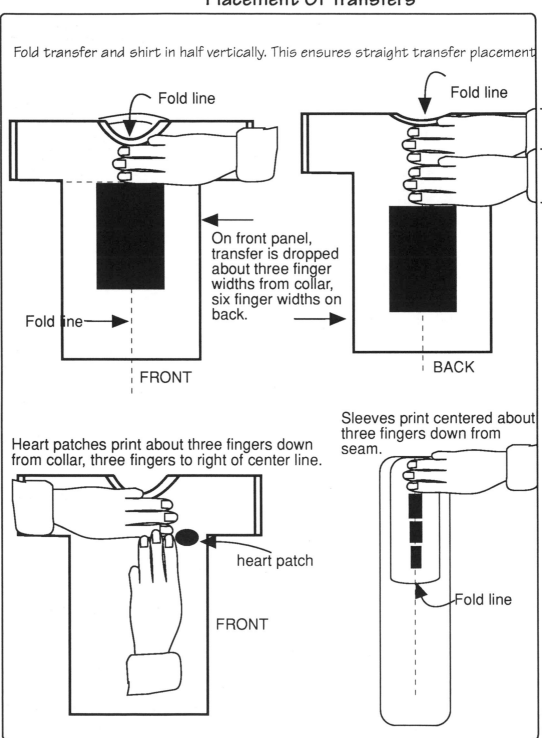

Fold transfer and shirt in half vertically. This ensures straight transfer placement

Fold line

Fold line

On front panel, transfer is dropped about three finger widths from collar, six finger widths on back.

Fold line →

FRONT

BACK

Heart patches print about three fingers down from collar, three fingers to right of center line.

heart patch

FRONT

Sleeves print centered about three fingers down from seam.

Fold line

Chapter 3

Copier Techniques For T'S

Just about any photocopier can be used to print a T-shirt design. When the artwork has few elements, such as a photo, the copier is quicker and faster to print from than a computer. The downside to the copier technique is the inability to modify or combine graphic elements easily.

However, the copier is the machine of choice when printing a large number of sheets with the same design.

Several copiers use a two-step method which requires two heat pressings, Most, however, use the simple one step method. Be certain to use the method appropriate to the copier you are using.

Running an incorrect transfer sheet through the copier could cause serious damage to the copier.

ONE-STEP COPIER METHOD

Most color copiers are capable of using the one-step method. Using this method, a special heat transfer sheet is fed through the machine just as you would a piece of copy paper. The transfer sheet is then heat pressed onto a garment.

Color copiers have become fairly common and can be found in many offices, quick-print shops, copy shops, office supply stores and even libraries. If you use one of these sources be sure to take along a transfer sheet. Few color copier owners have these sheets on hand. Canon brand Color copier

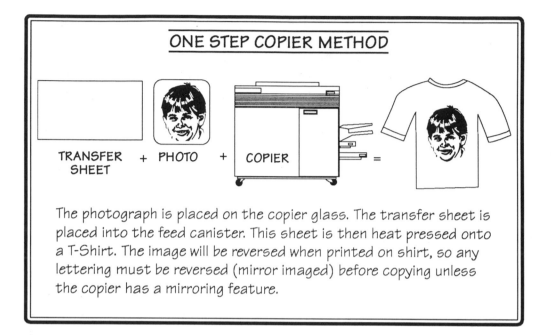

ONE STEP COPIER METHOD

TRANSFER   +   PHOTO   +   COPIER   =
SHEET

The photograph is placed on the copier glass. The transfer sheet is placed into the feed canister. This sheet is then heat pressed onto a T-Shirt. The image will be reversed when printed on shirt, so any lettering must be reversed (mirror imaged) before copying unless the copier has a mirroring feature.

outlets near you can be found by calling the Canon Company at 1-800-652-2666. Check with your copier dealer before using heat transfers on other brands of color copiers.

Color copier transfer sheets in various sizes are readily available from a number of specialty dealers. See the *Resources* section at the back of the book for names of transfer vendors.

TWO-STEP COPIER METHOD

Some color copier owners may be hesitant to run the coated transfer sheet through their machine. In this case, or if you are using a black-print-only copier, you can use the two-step method.

Step 1.

    Photo copy your artwork onto a plain sheet of paper.

Step 2.

    Using heat and pressure, transfer the image on the plain

sheet of paper onto a special transfer sheet. This sheet is then heat pressed onto the garment.

It is not necessary to reverse the graphic you are using. The graphic created on the copier will be mirrored when heat pressed onto the transfer sheet and mirrored again when the transfer sheet is pressed onto the garment.

All one-color copiers use the two-step method. See Resources for dealers specializing in these transfers.

PREPARING ARTWORK:

Many T-shirt graphics can be copied onto a transfer without any further preparation. A photo of your pet, for example.

Combining the photo with other elements will require you to make a "paste-up". For T-shirt artwork a paste-up is simply a sheet of white paper the size of your copier paper on which you paste or tape the graphic elements. For example, if you want to add your pet's name under their photo, simply attach the name to the paste-up underneath the photo. If you use the one-step method, the wording must be mirrored (written backwards). No need to do this in the two-step method.

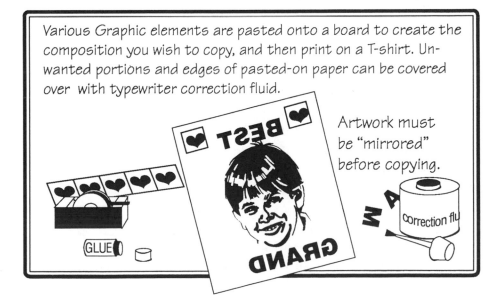

Various Graphic elements are pasted onto a board to create the composition you wish to copy, and then print on a T-shirt. Unwanted portions and edges of pasted-on paper can be covered over with typewriter correction fluid.

Artwork must be "mirrored" before copying.

When using the paste-up method, elements from many sources can be brought together.

While you can touch-up unwanted marks on the completed transfer it is a lot easier to clean up the artwork before photocopying. Ordinary office whiteout works well for covering unwanted marks and the edges of pasted art elements.

ART SOURCES FOR COPIER T-SHIRTS

Lettering - Computer generated; hand drawn; stencils; rubdown; cut out of magazine.

Clip Art - Computer software; clip art books; (check the local library, plus art, craft and office supply stores)

Drawings - on computer; scan in; hand draw

Photos-Old, new; Put her head on his body!; photos from magazines, yearbooks, etc.

Cartoons - Draw; scan; copy

Objects-Hand; feet; pencil; etc. placed on glass surface of copier

---

(Much of the information in the rest of this chapter is repeated from Chapter 2, T-shirts from your computer. It is presented again to eliminate the necessity of jumping back and forth in the manual.)

Using the One-Step Copier Method

Transferring your photocopied image into the shirt fabric is accomplished by heat and pressure. The amount of pressure and heat to apply is determined by several variables such as: Type of fabric to be pressed, type of transfer sheet being applied, and type of pressing equipment being used.

T-shirt fabric is either 100% cotton or a blend of cotton and a synthetic such as polyester. All transfer sheets will print onto Cotton blends, a few will work with 100% cotton. Both fabrics require about the same amount of heat and pressure. However, non-cotton fabrics vary dramatically. Heat Transfer manufacturers usually suggest proper heat and pressure settings. Nevertheless, non-cotton fabrics should be test pressed on a scrap piece of cloth before pressing your final design.

Heat and pressure settings vary somewhat between Heat Transfer Sheet manufacturers. Follow their directions, but again, do a test run on a scrap of cloth.

Be extremely careful not to move the transfer on the shirt once the transfer or shirt is hot. Moving the transfer will create smears on your shirt.

An ordinary household iron set to a cotton setting (do not use steam) will work great with just about any transfer. This will probably be the only heat press you will ever need. If, however, you plan to do a large number of shirts or find you need a more sophisticated method, then you will need to look into accessing a Heat Press. Many heat transfer manufacturers do not recommend using a hand iron with their transfers. They believe only a commercial heat press will do an adequate pressing.

A Heat Press is essentially an iron with a large heat surface. The garment is placed onto the platform (ironing board), the transfer is placed on top of the garment, and the top (iron) is closed down against the platform. This system allows the transfer sheet to be pressed and heated in one step. The heat press has temperature and pressure adjustments.

A Heat Press sells in the $400 to $1000 neighborhood. Used presses are sometimes listed in classified ads of local newspapers and screenprinting trade journals. In some large cities you can rent these presses. Or, you might want to farm the work out. There is someone in your area who has a heat press. In a large metropolitan area there may be hundreds. A small T-shirt shop is the best bet. Most heat press owners will do your pressing for a nominal fee.

A Photo Mounting Press, a piece of equipment used by photographers, can be used in place of a heat press. While you have to do your own timing and other adjustments manually, this equipment is able to do a very good job of T-shirt pressing.

Remove the paper:

After pressing the Heat Transfer Sheet into the shirt fabric, remove it by picking loose a corner and peeling the transfer from fabric using firm, steady pressure. Transfers must be peeled immediately while still hot. If it appears your transfer will not peel off easily and in one piece, reapply heat with a firm pressure being certain that the iron covers all edges and corners. The transfer should now peel off easily.

Using the Two-Step Copier Method

Run paper A through your copier. It is not necessary to reverse your graphics, as this is accomplished in the process using paper B.

Use very high pressure to assure a complete transfer of the image. Temperature should be at about 350 degrees F.

Place paper A (image up) on a padded press with paper B aligned on top. Cover with a heavy sheet of paper and press for 5 seconds. Place hot, bonded papers on hard surface and rub briefly with a cloth to remove trapped air pockets. Peel apart when cool. The image now appears on paper B and any excess paper should be trimmed from around it.

Place the item to be imaged on the press and position paper B on it, with the image facing down. Press 5 second and peel hot.

CAUTION: Heat transfers can be applied with a household iron, but some, such as opaque and copier transfers, take a bit of skill. The pressure you apply must be consistent over the entire transfer and heat must be kept close to the manufacturere's suggested heat setting.

Practice on scrap fabric before you do your final pressing.

Many heat transfer manufacturers do not recommend using a household iron to apply any of their transfers. They suggest their transfers be applied only with a commercial heat press. If you chose this route, see the "Heat Press" section in chapter 2 for sources and workarounds.

Chapter 4

The
Nitty
Gritty

Here is the nitty-gritty, the down in the trenches "How To".

    <u>Don't throw this manual away</u> after you learn how to make T-shirts with the printer you currently own. Things change. A few months from now you may be printing from an entirely different printer! Or what about all the people who will need your technical support? Or what if you want more colors, or a larger print? What would happen if you lost the manual the day before you were given a scanner or your friend loaned you a camcorder for the rest of your life? What if the software you now have could be updated for free and included new capabilities you never even heard of before? What if, what if?—<u>KEEP THE MANUAL</u>!

WARNING: *Failure to keep this manual in a safe place could be hazardous to your future fun.*

    Specifics of transfer printing and pressing differ according to the printer used, the method of printing, the pressing equipment and the transfer material manufacturer. Following the instructions for your printer as presented in this chapter will give you the optimum results from the combination of equipment and materials used. Do not let the detail overwhelm you. The process will seem natural after you do your first shirt.

PICKING A PRINTER METHOD

If you have access to a <u>color printer</u>, your decision of which way to go is simple—there is only one way, the heat transfer sheet method.

<u>Laser printers</u> present a choice: use a special cartridge or special transfer paper. With the cartridge, printing is simple and clean, can be output in several colors and requires no special paper. But a cartridge isn't cheap! The alternative is the special transfer sheet. Sheets are less expensive than cartridges, but require two pressings. Either method will get the job done, you just need to decide which way is best for you.

<u>Dot Matrix</u> printers also require you to choose. Special ribbons on plain paper have the benefit of using several colors by switching (and first buying) different colored ribbons. Transfer sheets using the regular printer ribbon is very easy to use, makes a good print but does not have the potential of several colors.

HEAT-PRESSURE SETTINGS.

How much pressure, how much heat do you need—it depends! Start with the recommended settings on your iron and moderate to heavy pressure. But this may not give you the results you want. Keep experimenting. The amount of heat and pressure to use is best found by trial and error. A little practice on scrap cloth will show you the best combination to use. When you discover the best combination, write it down in your little black book or other appropriate never to be lost document. If you don't write it down, next month you may have to do the whole practice thing over again!

Using a Wax Thermal Printer and INK JETS (Bubbble Jets)

To print T-shirts on a wax thermal or ink jet printer, simply substitute the regular paper in the feeder tray with the special heat transfer paper—the regular ribbon is used. Heat press the printed transfer onto a shirt and be ready to be amazed! The quality is excellent.

Printing on a wax thermal or ink jet allows you to design your shirts using millions of color, and you need print only one shirt, but you can print thousands if you wish. Since there is no changing of ribbons or cartridges, the wax thermal or ink jet is ideal for high-quality quick shirt prints. (also see Ink Jet w/Cartridge below)

These machines are available in 8 1/2" x 11", 8 1/2" x 14", and 11" x 17" print sizes. Most machines use a "gripper" clamp to pull the paper through the print head. This gripper area is unprintable so an 8 1/2" x 11" sheet has a reduced print area. If you are having someone else doing your printout, be sure to find out the "printable" area before designing your shirt.

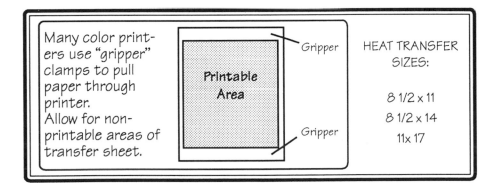

Before printing, "mirror" image your graphic either on screen or by selecting "mirror", "emulsion down" , or whatever your print driver uses to mirror the printed image. The mirrored printed graphic will again be mirrored when it is pressed onto the shirt, making it "right reading". Wax thermal transfer sheets are readily available from most specialty vendors. Those listed in the *Resource* section all carry this transfer sheet.

USING A DYE SUBLIMATION PRINTER

Printing a T-shirt on a dye-sublimation printer requires two steps. First, print your graphic onto a sheet of paper. Heat press this sheet onto a special transfer sheet. This transfer sheet is then heat pressed onto the shirt. This is a bit more work than the wax thermal process, but your effort will be rewarded with very bright, vivid colors. Like the wax thermal, millions of colors are available. You can print only one shirt or thousands if you wish.

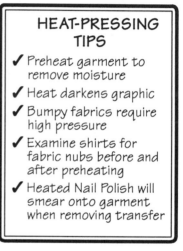

HEAT-PRESSING TIPS

✓ Preheat garment to remove moisture

✓ Heat darkens graphic

✓ Bumpy fabrics require high pressure

✓ Examine shirts for fabric nubs before and after preheating

✓ Heated Nail Polish will smear onto garment when removing transfer

The image does not need to be "mirrored" when printing because the image will be reversed when it is pressed onto the transfer sheet, and made "right reading" when pressed onto the shirt.

Dye sub heat transfer sheets are readily available and can be purchased from the vendors listed in the *Resource* section at the end of the manual, or possibly from the printer's manufacturer.

USING A LASER PRINTER *AND* INK JETS - *WITH CARTRIDGE*

The special toner cartridge will print a large number of shirt transfers and is available in several colors. Check resource section for dealers who specialize in these cartridges.

To print, substitute the special cartridge for the printer's normal cartridge. Print onto regular paper as you normally would. Mirror the image–Flip it horizontally to read correctly after transferring to shirt. This can be done on your computer by flipping your image on the screen before printing or by reversing on the printer by setting your "print" dialogue box for "reverse", "mirror image", or "emulsion down"

Take the printed sheet and place it face down on the shirt. Place a sheet of paper or a paper bag on top of the transfer to mask it and the fabric from the iron. Press firmly for 20 seconds. Lift the iron gently, reposition the iron, and press firmly for 5 seconds. Larger transfer will require more motion with the iron. Allow the transfer to cool completely before removing paper.

When you have several images repeated on a page, space them out so that they use the toner evenly across the page rather than placing them all in a line. Small print and details will not transfer well to rough surfaces such as T-Shirts. Smooth surfaces, such as metal, will show fine details very well. If using a color ribbon, copy will appear black on the paper. When transferred to the fabric surface it shows true colors.

Fabrics high in polyester work best, although most fabrics with a smooth tight weave will work, 50/50 or 80/20 polyester/cotton work well. Lighter colored fabrics show off the image with greater contrast. Thicker materials and double knits have more area for transfer and produce richer results.

> ### LASER COLOR
> Dye Sublimation Laser Toner cartridges are available in an array of colors. Use these cartridges for jobs that require several separate colors, like red, green, blue. For full color jobs such as photographs, you will need to buy four cartridges: magenta, cyan, yellow, black. By passing your artwork through the printer once for each color, the combination creates potentially millions of colors.

USING A LASER PRINTER *WITH HEAT TRANSFER PAPER*

This method requires two-steps. First print out your graphic on a plain sheet of paper. This sheet is then heat pressed onto a heat transfer sheet. The transfer sheet is then heat pressed onto the garment.

Run paper "A" through your printer. It is not necessary to reverse your graphics, as this is accomplished in the process using paper "B".

> Running an incorrect transfer sheet through the laser printer could cause very serious damage to the printer.

Use very high pressure to assure a complete transfer of the image. Hand Iron temperature should be at about 350 degrees F. Set heat press to 350 on high pressure setting. Pad the platen if additional pressure is required.

Place paper "A" (image up) on a padded press with paper "B" aligned on top. Cover with a sheet of paper and press for 5 seconds.

Place these hot, bonded papers on hard surface and rub briefly with a cloth to remove trapped air pockets. Peel apart when cool. The image now appears on paper "B" and any excess paper should be trimmed from around the printed graphic.

Place the item to be imaged, such as a T-shirt, on the padded press and position paper "B" on it, with the image facing down. Press five second and peel transfer while still hot.

USING A DOT MATRIX PRINTER *WITH HEAT TRANSFER PAPER*

Feed the heat transfer paper into the printer so that the textured (rougher) surface receives the print. Adjust the paper to leave a minimum top and side margin of 1/4". Print your graphics.

When printing letters or numbers, reverse print (mirror image). This can be done by flipping the image on the screen or using "mirror image", "emulsion down" or "reverse image" in the printing dialogue box before printing.

When printing with a brand new ribbon you may want to use the draft option (if applicable) to avoid smearing. You can also use the paper thickness lever to position the printhead further away from the paper. Also, due to the limitations of dot matrix printers, you may get small white lines running through your solid colors. This usually disappears when your printout is transferred onto the fabric.

If your printer is limited to single color capability, you can add color with ordinary wax crayons or felt markers directly onto the transfer surface before ironing. Once ironed, both the crayoned area and the computer print will transfer in washproof color onto the fabric.

Cut away excess (unprinted) portion of transfer paper, leaving at least 1/4" around graphics. Set iron to "dry" cotton setting. Fold a pillowcase in half and place it on a glass or formica surface. Do not use ironing board. Place garment onto pillowcase making certain entire area to receive transfer is resting squarely over the wrinkle-free pillowcase. Center transfer, printed side down, onto the garment making certain all four edges are also over the pillowcase.

Press preheated iron firmly onto the transfer for 12 seconds in each of the six positions. (see illustration) Immediately reheat entire surface by making 3 complete circles with the iron over the transfer, being certain that the iron covers all edges and corners. Use firm pressure when reheating.

Quickly place iron aside and, beginning in one corner, peel transfer from fabric using firm, steady pressure.

Gently smooth the fabric with your hands and allow to cool for 10 seconds.

USING A DOT MATRIX PRINTER *WITH RIBBON*

Reverse the image on the screen (mirror image) Turn off your printer. Install the special heat transfer ribbon. Be careful to get the ribbon between the guideplates. Choose the print option that makes the darkest transfer. However, with a brand new ribbon you may want to use the print draft option (if applicable) to avoid smearing. You can also use the paper thickness lever to position the printhead further away from the paper. When you are finished, remove the special ribbon and store it in a recloseable bag. This ribbon is not suitable for normal printing.

Cover one end of your ironing board with a 1'x2' sheet of aluminum foil to protect it from the heat and ink. Put the shirt around the end of the board so only the front half is on top of the foil, otherwise some ink might bleed through to the back surface.

Center the printed transfer ink side down on top of the shirt. Cover this with a double thickness of blank paper to distribute the heat and keep the shirt from scorching (the top sheet of blank paper will probably scorch during the ironing). Be sure the foil, transfer and blank paper are lined up and free of wrinkles.

Place iron firmly on the top sheet of paper (your iron should never touch the T-shirt) and hold for approximately 20 seconds. The area you are working with should not be larger than twice the "footprint" of the iron. If you have a larger transfer, cut it in pieces and iron them on separately. Do not let the paper slide as you iron, or the image will be smeared. Practice on old T-shirts or cloth, by selecting a suitable temperature on your iron from medium to high. Use 50/50 blend, cotton-polyester for best results, as 100% cotton will fade quicker. Higher percentage polyester cloth (up to a maximum of 65%) can be used if you are careful during ironing. (100% cotton can be used if the garment's transfer area is first sprayed with a polyester based liquid. This spray is sold by most vendors listed under Dye-Sublimation in Resource section)

See Chapter 2 for information and illustrations on placement and heat pressing garments.

TRANSFER SERVICE

If for one reason or another you want someone else to make your T-shirts, the Black Lightning company in Vermont will do it for you—all of the work or a part of it.

Send them a disk and they will put your design on transfers which they will send to you for you to heat press; or they will press the transfer onto shirts for you. If you are really feeling lazy, they will even design the shirt for you.

They can also put your designs on mugs, metal, caps and a bunch of other stuff.

Black Lightning 1-800-252-2599

THERMAL TRANSFER SHEETS

Listed here are the primary sources for accessing heat transfers. These suppliers will help you find exactly what you need. Additional suppliers are listed in the Resource section in Appendix.

Laser Printer
Thermal Transfer Sheets

RAMCO Computer Supplies
455 Grove
Manteno, IL 60950
1-815-480-8081

Double Exposure
69 Main Street
Vincentown, NJ 08088
1-800-526-2822

QLT
95 Morton Street
New York, NY 10014
1-800-221-9832

Dot Matrix
Thermal Transfer Sheets

Foto-Wear
101 Pocono Drive
Milford, PA 18337
1-717-296-4709

RAMCO Computer Supplies
455 Grove
Manteno, IL 60950
1-815-480-8081

Double Exposure
69 Main Street
Vincentown, NJ 08088
1-800-526-2822

Dye-Sublimation
Thermal Transfer Sheets

Double Exposure
69 Main Street
Vincentown, NJ 08088
1-800-526-2822

Wyndstone
236 Egidi Drive, Ste A
Wheeling, IL 60090
1-800-395-8870

Foto-Wear
101 Pocono Drive
Milford, PA 18337
1-717-296-4709

Wax Thermal
Thermal Transfer Sheets

Double Exposure
69 Main Street
Vincentown, NJ 08088
1-800-526-2822

Wyndstone
236 Egidi Drive, Ste A
Wheeling, IL 60090
1-800-395-8870

Foto-Wear
101 Pocono Drive
Milford, PA 18337
1-717-296-4709

Ink Jet
Thermal Transfer Sheets

Double Exposure
69 Main Street
Vincentown, NJ 08088
1-800-526-2822

Wyndstone
236 Egidi Drive, Ste A
Wheeling, IL 60090
1-800-395-8870

Foto-Wear
101 Pocono Drive
Milford, PA 18337
1-717-296-4709

PhotoCopier
Thermal Transfer Sheets

Double Exposure
69 Main Street
Vincentown, NJ 08088
1-800-526-2822

Wyndstone
236 Egidi Drive, Ste A
Wheeling, IL 60090
1-800-395-8870

Foto-Wear
101 Pocono Drive
Milford, PA 18337
1-717-296-4709

LASER THERMAL CARTRIDGES

Black Lightening
Riddle Pond Road
West Topsham, VT 05086
1-800-252-2599

RAMCO Computer Supplies
455 Grove
Manteno, IL 60950
1-815-480-8081

HEAT PRESS LOCATIONS

In addition to the list of places to access a heat press already noted in the text, the following companies have heat presses in many stores for customer use. Check your telephone yellow pages or call their 800 number for the outlet nearest you.

Kinko 1-800-743-COPY

Staples Office Supplies 1-617-229-0369

(Check with your office supply store as many stores plan to add this service.

The following companies can refer you to their heat press owner closest to you.

INSTA Graphic Systems
1-800-421-6971

HIX
1-800-835-0606

Geo Knight & Co
1-800-525-6766

STAHL'S
1-800-521-9702

Lancer Graphics (Canada)
1-800-263-1609

(HIX, INSTA and Knight also manufacturer hat and mug presses.)

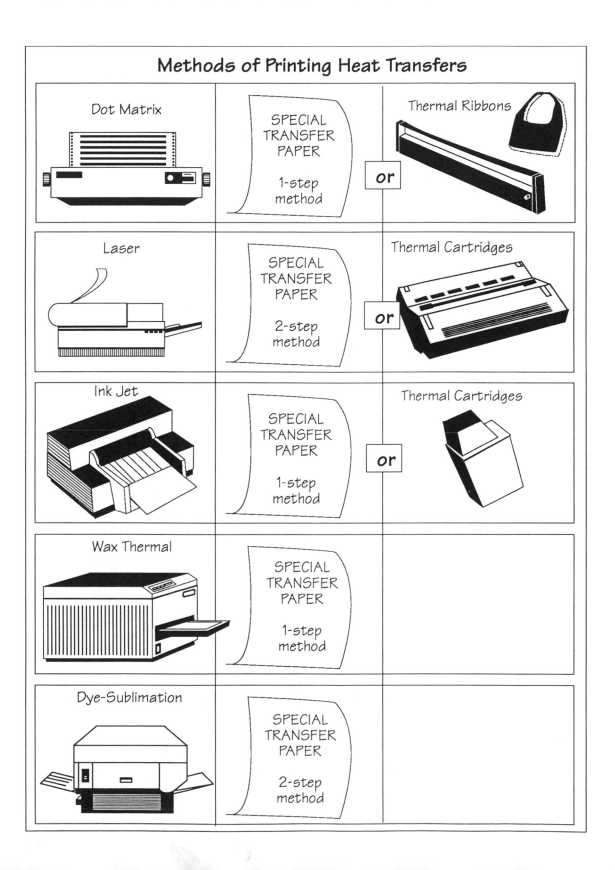

Methods of Printing Heat Transfers

Dot Matrix	SPECIAL TRANSFER PAPER 1-step method	**or** Thermal Ribbons
Laser	SPECIAL TRANSFER PAPER 2-step method	**or** Thermal Cartridges
Ink Jet	SPECIAL TRANSFER PAPER 1-step method	**or** Thermal Cartridges
Wax Thermal	SPECIAL TRANSFER PAPER 1-step method	
Dye-Sublimation	SPECIAL TRANSFER PAPER 2-step method	

GRAPHICS IDEAS CAN BE FOUND MOST ANYWHERE

Ordinary, everyday things can be an effective means of communicating an idea that must be grasped quickly. And they are easy to draw or configure from computer dingbats and clip art.

A stop sign leaves little question as to its meaning. ⇨

Adding an unexpected message to the ordinary graphic can have great impact.

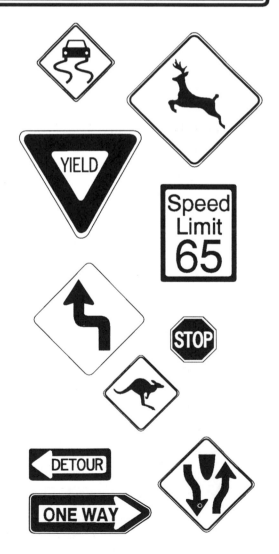

Chapter 5

Putting Photographs On T-Shirts

Photographs printed on T-shirts have unlimited possibilities and their graphic impact cannot be matched by any other technique. Only a few years ago printing a photo T-shirt was very expensive and required specialized equipment. But today anyone can print a photo T and do it better than was possible even five years ago.

The three methods to print photo T's are:

1. Computer generated
2. Color Copier Technique
3. Screenprinting

COMPUTER GENERATED PHOTO T'S

The computer method of generating a photo T-shirt is the most versatile of the three methods. The photo can be manipulated endlessly to give you possibilities limited only by your imagination. Additionally, the computer method allows you to combine several photos, or combine photos with other types of graphics making a new piece of art. Lettering, clip art, drawings, or hundreds of other elements can be added to the photo graphic. (see illustration on facing page for a sampling of the possibilities)

The first occasion most people witnessed an example of digitizing was the awesome photos send back to earth from the first lunar landing. The government paid billions for this technology; today it costs only hundreds of dollars.

DIGITIZING:

Photos are brought into the computer by a process call "digitizing". Essentially, digitizing translates various shades of black or color into numbers—*digits*. The photo is divided into extremely minute parts called pixels. Depending upon the resolution of the digitizing device, the number of pixels in one square inch can be as high as thousands. Each of these pixels is assigned a number (digit) and the computer assigns a number to each pixel according to its position on the photo and its intensity (dark/light). Computers can understand this numbering system and process the digits at lightning speed. The numbers are translated back again into shades of gray when your computer sends its numbers to the printer or monitor which both use the same numbering system.

Our way of "seeing" has a parallel to digitizing. Like a camera lens, our eyes react to degrees of light and separate this light into a range of bright to dark, or to various shades of black or color (a type of digitizing). Our brain puts all this together and matches this information to what it has stored away from previous experience, and then identifies this pattern or range of shades as a tree or the face of George Washington.

DIGITIZING DEVICES

You will need to use a digitizing device to bring the digits of a photo into your computer. These devices fall into three categories: Scanners, Video grab boards and CD disks.

Scanners:

The most common digitizing device is the computer scanner. Scanners are available from a number of vendors and in various configurations. All scanners are capable of bringing a photo into the computer. They differ in how they do this, how well they do this and by the type of photo they are able to digitize.

The flatbed scanner can digitize reflective art (like photos in your family album). Flatbeds have a glass surface on which the

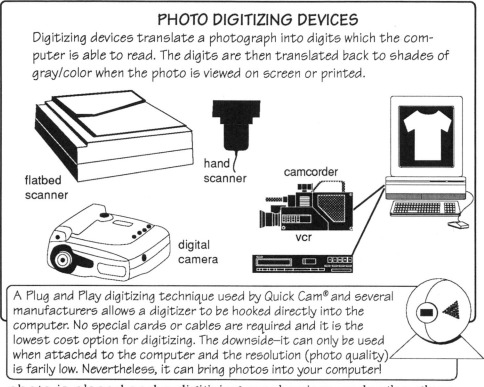

PHOTO DIGITIZING DEVICES

Digitizing devices translate a photograph into digits which the computer is able to read. The digits are then translated back to shades of gray/color when the photo is viewed on screen or printed.

flatbed scanner

hand scanner

camcorder

vcr

digital camera

A Plug and Play digitizing technique used by Quick Cam® and several manufacturers allows a digitizer to be hooked directly into the computer. No special cards or cables are required and it is the lowest cost option for digitizing. The downside—it can only be used when attached to the computer and the resolution (photo quality) is farily low. Nevertheless, it can bring photos into your computer!

photo is placed and a digitizing mechanism under the glass scans the photo. The operation looks similar to that of a photocopier. Flatbeds can be either black and white capable only or full color capable.

The quality of a flatbed scanned photo is usually sufficient for T-shirts. Scanners are sold with resolutions ranging up to more than 6000 dots per inch (dpi). Theoretically, this high resolution will produce a better photo scan than say a 300 dpi scanner. In actuality, 300 dpi, or lower, is more than sufficient for most T-shirt photos. The additional dpi resolution creates huge files which are more difficult to work with and may not even print unless you have a mega-memory printer.

Unless your flatbed has a special attachment it cannot digitize negatives, slides or 35mm film. For these items a specialized <u>slide scanner</u> is needed. Some of these scanners can handle 35mm film only, some can handle any type of non-reflective photos. This type of equipment is sold by Leaf, Microtek and Canon, to name a few.

A hand-held scanner performs the same functions as the flatbed scanner. When using this type of scanner the photo remains stationary while the scanner operator moves the scanner across the photo. These scanners cost far less than flatbeds. However, before you decide to buy one of these scanners you should try one out to determine if the low cost cancels out the limitations of these devices. Many steady-handed people are very happy with the hand-held scan solution.

If you don't have access to a scanner or the type of scanner you need for the job, for a small fee you can have your photo digitized by many local or mail order office services or computer service bureau.

Digital Boards:

Another digitizing method attaches a special interface onto the computer which digitizes incoming photos from camcorders, video players or television sets. These digitizing computer boards, also known as video grabbers, are sold by several manufacturers. Color Snap and Computer Eyes are two of the many brands available. These boards are installed in the computer and wired to the camcorder or other device from which you want to capture photos. Once the photo is "grabbed" it can be used like a photo which has been digitized by other methods.

Still Video Camera:

Still another method to import photos is the special digitizing cameras, sometimes called still video cameras. With this camera, the picture you snap is digitized and then recorded on a diskette which can be put into your computer to read. Two such cameras are Xapshot and Apple Quick Take.

Photo CD:

If you have a lot of photos, like each family member and their pets, and you have a CDRom attached to your computer, you might want to have the photos put on a CD. For a rather reasonable cost, authorized Kodak outlets will put all your photos on a CD disk. When you get the disk back you will have all your photos digitized at three or four (low to high) resolutions. These photos can be used on your computer in the same way you use other photo digitizer methods. Kodak also includes a thumbnail printout of all the photos they have put on your disk. Call 1-800-242-2424 for a dealer in your area, or LASERQUICK, 1-800-477-2679 by mail.

Photo CD's can be used over and over again for many applications.

Beyond using your family photo CD for T-shirts, you can put these pictures in a multimedia show, use them as a computer screensaver, or print them out as part of a family newsletter, Christmas cards, wanted posters and a zillion other things.

Any of the "canned" photos CD's available from vendors can be used on Shirts much like you would use clip art.

> If you do not own or have access to one of the digitizing devices, many local service bureau-type companies are offering this service. By mail, one of the best deals is Seattle Film Works. They can put a roll of film, existing slides or negatives on on a floppy disk (up to 36) for a very reasonable cost.
> Seattle Film Works • 1260 16th Ave W • Seattle, WA 98119 * 1-800-445-3348

COPIER METHOD FOR PHOTOS

If you do not have access to any of these computer input devices there is still a way to get that photo on a T-shirt—the copier. For specifics, see the section "*Copier Techniques*". Essentially, it works this way. Place a photo on the copier glass and copy it onto a special copier transfer which you have placed in the feeder tray. For a black and white photo you can use your office copier. For color, have it printed by a copy shop with a color laser copier-check with them first, you may have to take along a copier transfer sheet.

SCREENPRINTING PHOTOS:

Screenprinting photos is expensive. But things are changing and this method may soon be competitive. Many screenprinters are becoming "process" capable. This method uses only four basic inks to produce millions of colors as opposed to the more traditional "spot color" method which prints only one color at a time and is not capable of blending together the many colors of a photograph. Thus, process color is necessary for photo screenprinting because a photo has thousands of color variations.

In addition to finding a process-color screenprinter, you will need to have your photo color-separated into the four process colors. This process is very expensive and therefore cost effective only if you are printing a large number of shirts. (for more information on this subject, refer to Chapter 9)

PHOTO TECHNIQUES

A digitized photo can be saved in several computer file formats (languages) according to the type of computer you are using. Check your manuals for the format of choice; if you hate reading those manuals, saving photos in tiff (.tif) will work on just about any computer. (A few programs, such as Word Perfect require graphics to be saved in their proprietary format. Fine, but there is no reason you can't save the file in several formats so it can be used everywhere!)

Photos can be *placed* or *imported* on most drawing and page layout programs along with more recent database and spreadsheet software plus many other types of programs. Most photos can be placed without any further corrective work; thus a photo manipulation program is not necessary unless you wish to alter the photo in some fashion.

Placed or imported photos cannot be manipulated. Any modi-

> ### COMMON USES FOR PHOTOS ON T-SHIRTS
>
> Collage
> Class Group Picture
> Individual Class Members
> Family Reunion Group Photo
> Pet Photos
> Old Photos
> Then and Now
> Jokes (Millions of them)
> Boat
> Horse
> Car
> Grandchildren
> Movie Star
> Sweetheart
> Report Card (good ones)
> Newspaper article
> Roasts
> Resume
> Things that defy description!

fying of the digitized photo must be done prior to placing it. Photo manipulation programs such as Adobe Photoshop and Corel Draw allow you to "clean up" a scan by lightening, darkening, sharpening and a host of other tweaking methods. When the photo is clean, the tweaked version is saved before importing/placing into the final graphic. Of course, the photo can be printed directly from the photo manipulation program if you wish.

Generally, photos should be made a tad lighter (as opposed to darker) than normal because the heat pressing process tends to darken the photo a tad.

PHOTO MANIPULATION

Most digital input devices capture their photo files as either RGB, CYMK, Bitmap, Gray Scale or line art. RGB and CMYK are color files, bitmap, gray scale and line art are black/white files.

RGB—Red, Green, Blue—has three channels or sublevels, one layer for each color. A computer color monitor creates all of its colors from these three base colors. For T-shirt photo work, the RGB method is fine as long as the printer works from only three colors (four color ribbons on some printers can't work with only these three colors, while others convert the three colors to the printer's ribbon colors—check the manual)

CMYK—Cyan, (blue) Magenta, (Red) Yellow, Black—is the color system used in the printing industry to produce full color printing. This system is also used to screenprint photos. If your digital input device saves files only in RGB you will have to convert the files to CMYK using a photo program such as Adobe Photoshop.

Bitmapped files are made up of pixels which are either black or white, with no in-between shades. Pixels within a gray scale file will fit in a range of zero black to 100% black (256 shades of black). Gray scale, RGB and CMYK files can be converted to a bitmapped file, but bitmaps can't be made into a gray scale.

Within the confines of your scanned file restrictions a photo manipulation program can do just about anything to improve or alter your digitized photo. (See illustration on facing page)

CUSTOMIZING PHOTOS

To made a T-shirt photo "pop", try to keep the subject as simple as possible. Here are a few of the hundreds of ways to do this.

sillhouette

ovalize

crop

homogenize

If the shirt story is about her, cut him out!

Can be done on computer in photo or drawing program. Use a rubylith if doing it without computer. If the photo is not valuable, simply cut out with a scissors.

Rubylith

Rubylith is a sheet of double layered acetate. One sheet is clear, the other red. Lay sheet over photo and simply cut out the portion you want to show. Rubylith is available in most art or craft stores

Sometimes, two heads are better than one!

MAKING BIG GRAPHICS FROM SMALL PARTS

You can make a shirt design appear to be huge by heat pressing graphic elements separately. The trick is to heat press each piece without second pressing another element.

The first transfer has the photo imprinted. **1**

Text is printed on second transfer. **2**

Cut text page apart. **3**

Heat press first transfer. **4**

Move first transfer to back of pressing area and heat press second transfer. **5**

Turn shirt around (tail goes into press) and heat press third transfer. **6**

An 8 1/2" x 11" transfer graphic is usually large enough for most T-shirt designs. If your transfer sheets are not large enough by themselves, combine two or more. Just about any graphic can be split onto two transfers and brought back together when heat pressing.

Two transfers heat pressed separately to make large graphic.

From this ↑
to this ───→
in one pinch!

A little "pinch" in
photo manipulation
programs can turn
beauty into beast!
Adobe Photoshop
was used here.

Above: The "water color" filter in
photo software was used to
give the photo a unique look.

Left: The photo was posterized,
removing all the grays leaving
only black or white pixels.

Before:

Above: The left and right sides of our faces
are different from each other. Here the
operator duplicated the left side of the face,
flipped it horizontally and then joined it to
the original left side. Thus, the two
"left-sided" face.

Left: The same technique was used for the
two right sides of the face.

Tracing a Photograph

Photographs can be manually traced in a drawing/paint program—or automatically in a special tracing program such as Adobe Streamline. This process converts a photograph with thousands of grey shades (or colors) into black or white (line drawing). You may wish to use this technique for the effect or for the benefit of having crisp lines and artwork which you can use to make other artwork.

For manual tracing, bring the digitized photo into your drawing/paint program and trace the highlignts. Try different styles of drawing such as lines only, filled segments, etc. to find the style that best suits the photo. NO DIGITIZER? Try this method: make a photocopy of the photo on an acetate sheet, place the sheet on the glass screen of your monitor and start drawing/tracing in a drawing/paint program. This is definitely low-tech, but you can get some really neat results.

In a tracing program (many drawing /paint programs have this feature) simply set the parameters for black/white and let the computer do the tracing.

Tracing Technique

(A) The photo (used on previous pages) was first manually traced in a drawing program. Instead of filling in the outlined sections as was done in "B", the outlines were filled with horizontal black lines.

(B) The photo was autotraced in a tracing program.

(C) A photocopy of the photo was placed on monitor screen and traced in a drawing program. First, the dark areas were outlined and then the outlined areas were filled.

(D) Traced photos, because they are line art, can easily be incorporated into clip art to tell a story.

(E) Drawing programs permit you to take the traced photo apart. Here the face was re arranged, but there are literatlly millions of things you can do with the technique.

ETCETERA

Cover photos were scanned on a Microtek scanner from reflective art (right out of someone's photo album) Page 62 photos were taken from a commercial CD. Photo at bottom of page 63, was snapped with a still digital camera. All other photos taken with a camcorder and frame-grabbed using ColorSnap.

Chapter 6

T's
To Draw and
Wear

This method of designing T-shirts is so easy and fail proof that you may want to have a few sheets handy for creating lightening quick designs. Draw-it, press it, wear it!

With T's To Draw and Wear you will never have to be caught without a gift. If you don't have a shirt handy, Giftwrap the transfer. The recipient will love the idea of pressing the design on their own shirt.

A blank T's To Draw and Wear transfer is a great gift for children. Wearing their own creation on a T-shirt ranks ten "wows!" higher than frig door display.

This transfer is readily available from several vendors. See the *Resources* section for a vendor near you.

There are two approaches to designing T's To Draw and Wear. The artwork can be:

1. Drawn directly on the transfer or

2. Traced onto the transfer.

Because the transfer art must be "mirrored", using the carbon paper technique makes the process much easier. You can, of course, mirror your art as you draw (that is, draw everything backwards).

USING THE DRAWING METHOD

Place the transfer, smooth side UP, onto a hard, smooth surface, such as glass or formica. Use a pencil to draw your design, on the smooth side of transfer. Erase if necessary to make changes.

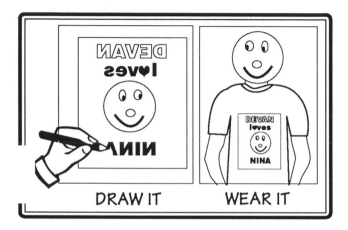

When you are pleased with the final design... place a sheet of carbon paper (carbon side UP) onto a smooth flat surface. Place the transfer directly over the carbon with your drawing facing UP. Using a ball point pen, and applying firm pressure, retrace your drawing (including words/numbers). Lift the transfer carefully and place the carbon paper aside for future use.

Turn the transfer over and place it back onto the hard, smooth surface with the carbon outline facing UP. The design (and words or numbers) will appear in reverse. This is correct. Using crayons, permanent markers or oil pastels, color in the reversed outline as you would color in a coloring book.

In a world of word processors and carbonless forms, carbon paper is going the way of the buggy whip and other items on the endangered species list. A few stores still have some stuffed away in a back room, often at the original 1970 price!

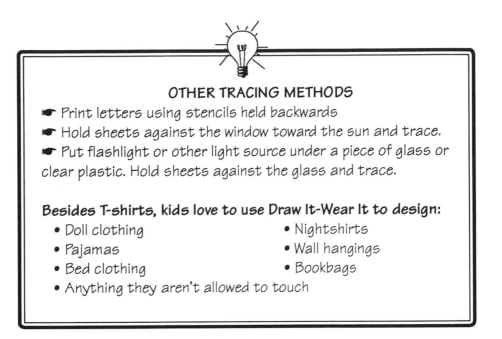

OTHER TRACING METHODS
☛ Print letters using stencils held backwards
☛ Hold sheets against the window toward the sun and trace.
☛ Put flashlight or other light source under a piece of glass or clear plastic. Hold sheets against the glass and trace.

Besides T-shirts, kids love to use Draw It-Wear It to design:
- Doll clothing
- Pajamas
- Bed clothing
- Anything they aren't allowed to touch
- Nightshirts
- Wall hangings
- Bookbags

USING THE TRACING METHOD:

Place carbon paper, carbon side UP, onto flat glass or formica surface Place the transfer rough side down, onto the carbon. Place the art you wish to trace directly over the transfer, with outline facing UP. Using a ball point pen, apply firm pressure and trace the design you have selected. This pressure will create an outline on the transfer. Turn the transfer with carbon outline facing UP and return it onto the smooth and hard surface. The design will appear in reverse. This is correct. Using ordinary crayons, permanent markers, or oil pastels, color in the outline as you would in a coloring book.

PRESSING

Preheat iron on "cotton" setting for 8 minutes. Do not use steam. Cut away excess (unprinted) portion of the transfer paper. Place garment onto pillowcase,

Children should not use hot irons without adult supervision

making certain transfer is resting squarely over a wrinkle-free pillowcase. Center transfer, printed side down onto the garment (making certain all four edges are also over the pillowcase). Press preheated iron firmly onto the transfer in each of the six positions (as illustrated) for 12 seconds each.

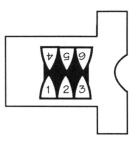

   Immediately reheat entire surface by making 3 complete circles with the iron over the transfer. Make sure the iron covers all edges and corners. Use firm pressure.

   Quickly place iron aside and, beginning in one corner, peel transfer from fabric using firm, steady pressure. If transfer does not peel, reheat surface again and try peeling.

Chapter 7

Low-Tech
T-Shirt
Makers

There are several low-tech methods used in designing T-shirts. Many of the methods do not require special training, equipment or supplies and can easily be used in the home. Other methods, such as embroidery, are best left to the people who specialize in that business.

Use these low-tech techniques alone or in combination with a computer generated design. For example, computer generate a graphic of a lion, but delete the eyes. In the eye space, heat press rhinestones—definitely an eye-popping shirt!

For the most part the materials used here have been greatly improved and are now readily available. Nevertheless, use caution in selecting the materials and the suppliers. There are still a few scoundrels around who will try to sell the leftovers from the old technology. Check the Resources section for a sampling of vendors who have proved to have good business practices. (This is not to be construed as an endorsement)

PRESSED-ON LETTERING:
There exists a huge assortment of ready-made lettering that can be pressed-on (heat glued) to garments. The quality of this new generation material is excellent, and the variety seemingly limitless.

The INSTA Graphics company in Cerritos, California is one of the biggest suppliers of this type of garment customizing. They offer lettering and numbering made from all sorts of material from plastic to chenille. If your project requires a dimensional look (like the varsity letters on college sweaters) press-on letters will be the least expensive way to go.

Pressed-on lettering is aligned on the shirt and then heat pressed.

If you are looking for something different, these same suppliers sell sprinkles, foil and rhinestones, all of which are heat pressed onto the garment creating a stunning effect.

In a class by itself is *puff*. Puff is a pressed-on type of thin, flat lettering that actually puffs (expands) into unique three dimensional letters when heated. Puff letters, sprinkles and sheets are also available in eye-popping neon.

Except for a few of the more exotic lettering materials, all you need to do is position the lettering on the garment and apply heat pressure. The manufacturer usually provides instructions on how to use their product. Pressed-on lettering can be a lot of fun and allows you to design some spectacular shirts that would not be possible with other methods..

HAND-PAINTING:

For the artistic, felt-tip dye markers, dye paint and assorted glue-based items can be applied directly onto a garment by hand. These materials are available in craft stores and craft catalogues. (Also see *Resources* section) Shirts crafted in this manner often require special care as they are a "craft" item and are not intended to take the abuse of everyday wear. But in the right hands, these shirts can become a piece of art!

A design can also be hand painted on a special heat transfer sheet (See T's To Draw and Wear Chapter). The advantage here is that mistakes don't have to be worn—just start over on a new transfer sheet.

Special Transfer Materials from INSTA Graphics:

Ultra-Span -   Stretches with the garment. Excellend for use on stretch fabrics such
                as used in leotards, wristbands, etc.

Foil -   Metallic foil which is heatpressed onto garments.

Puff -   Dimensional letters that puff (expand) when heat applied.

Tuff-Trans -   Adheres to nylon, vinyl, mesh.

Insta-Glo -   It shines in the dark!

Custom Transfer Service - Send them your artwork and they will create heat transfers
                for you. Actually, they will even do the artwork for you.

Insta Graphic Systems
13925 E.166th St
Ceritos, CA 90702
1-800-421-6971

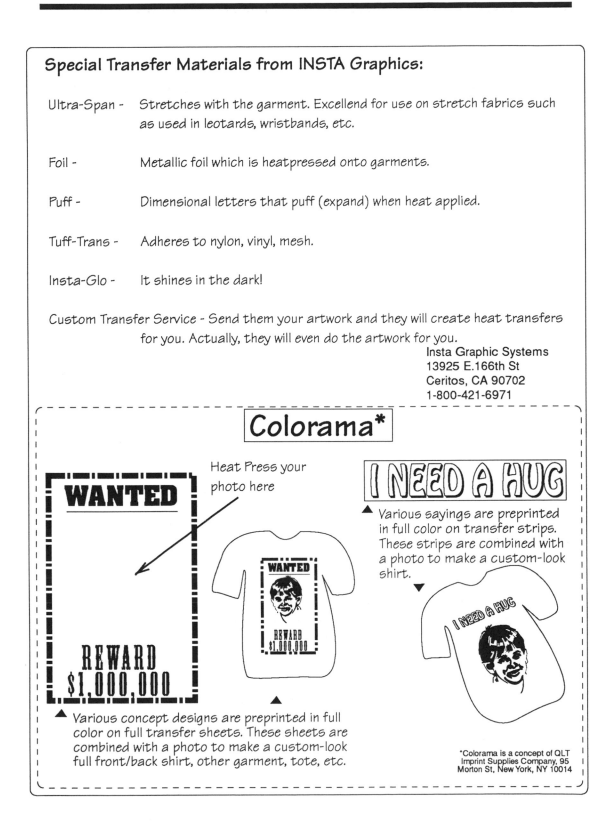

Colorama*

Heat Press your photo here

Various concept designs are preprinted in full color on full transfer sheets. These sheets are combined with a photo to make a custom-look full front/back shirt, other garment, tote, etc.

Various sayings are preprinted in full color on transfer strips. These strips are combined with a photo to make a custom-look shirt.

*Colorama is a concept of QLT Imprint Supplies Company, 95 Morton St, New York, NY 10014

APPLIQUE

Silhouettes or other shapes are cut from pieces of fabric such as felt. The fabric cutout is then sewn or glued onto a garment. Since this method falls under the heading "craft", look for the necessary materials in craft stores and catalogues. These creations require special care when laundering.

The term applique is also used by pressed-on lettering manufactures to describe a type of dimensional material which is heat pressed onto shirts.

SILHOUETTING
Outline the main parts of a photo then fill in with solid black. This can be done in computer photo manipulation programs or drawing programs. Or, simply overlay tracing or acetate paper and hand draw the outline.

STOCK TRANSFERS

These are ready-made heat transfers created by starving artists temporarily employed by companies in this business. (It has been rumored Michelangelo got his start here) Stock transfers are ready to be pressed onto your shirt the minute they arrive in the mail.

The variety and number of subjects covered is staggering. If you are concerned about wearing the same design as a few thousand other nice people, you can make a quasi-custom look by combining the stock transfer with other techniques such as pressed-on letters.

A few vendors stock huge inventories (10,000 different designs, one vendor touts) of these preprinted transfers and will send you a catalogue from which to order. A few vendors will

Stock Transfers and Preprints

"Stock Transfers" are heat transfers which already have a design printed on them. You press the transfer onto your own garment. "Preprints" are T-shirts with a design already printed on the garment. The below listed sources carry both Stock and Preprints.

CHRISTIAN
Solid Light
P.O.Box 261403
Columbus, OH 43226
1-800-726-9606

FISHING
Red Sky
PO Box 130
Ocean City, MD 21842
1-800-634-4354

MILITARY
New World
207 Union Street
Hackensack, NJ 07601
1-800-237-8901

These suppliers carry a large assortment of Stock Transfers from various manufacturers.

BEACH
Blondie Resort Wear
305 Racetrack Road, NE
Ft. Walton Beach, FL 32547
1-800-326-4889

FLORAL
LTD Impressions
580 N. Redwood Road
N. Salt Lake, UT 84054
1-800-292-7564

NAUTICAL
Next Graphic
1975 N.W. 18th Street
PompanoBeach, FL 3309
1-800-637-6398

BOO-Z WAREHOUSE
7119 Louisville Road
Salvisa KY 40372
1-800-552-4439

CAR/TRUCK
Thunder Island
47 West 34th Street
New York, NY 10001
1-212-947-8155

HAND PAINTED
Applied Arts
675 Anita Street
Chula Vista, CA 91911
1-619-575-5303

WESTERN
Sunrise Turquoise
520 Marnott Drive
Clarksville, IN 47129
1-800-874-7096

DISCOUNT TRANSFER
10420 Plano Rd
Dallas TX 75238
1-800-527-7060

COLLEGIATE
Bodek and Rhodes
2951 Grant Ave
Philadelphia, PA 19114
1-800-523-2721

HOLIDAY
Air Waves
6575 Huntley Road
Columbus, OH 43229
1-800-478-7335

NATURE
T Shirt Trivia
1419 West Park Drive
Little Rock, AR 72204
1-800-874-7096

MOUNTAIN GRAPHICS
485 N 1200 West
Lindon, UT 84042
1-800-473-9270

ENVIRONMENTAL
Native Sun
2828 20Th Avenue, North
St Petersburg, FL 33713
1-813-777-5800

HUMOROUS
Peppermint Tees
20 Jay Street
Brooklyn, NY 11201
1-800-253-8008

SPORTS
ProWorld
1511 Lancer Drive
Moorestown, NJ 08057
1-800-678-8289

IMPULSE WEAR
225 Business Cntr Dr
Blacklick, OH 43004
1-800-255-1280

ETHNIC/CULTRUAL
Solar Trans
608 New York Avenue
Wildwood, NJ 08260
1-800-257-8640

JUVENILE
Sea Dog Sportswear
PO Box 999
Oneco, FL 34264
1-813-351-0304

RESORT
Rag Tops
500 Electric Arenue
Farmington, NM 8741
1-800-772-5358

FINE ART
Philadelphia T-Shirt Museum
235 N 12th Street
Philadelphia, PA 19107
1-800-345-6173

MESSAGES
Stafford Blane Designs
3912 Dight Ave South
Minneopolis, MN 55406
1-800-326-2402

ANIMAL
Pure Art
7419 E. Helm Drive
Scottsdale, AZ 85260
1-800-727-4278

sell you only one while other vendors have a minimum of 12 or whatever. If you are looking for a special category of designs, such as Harley Davidson Logos, be diligent—somebody is selling it somewhere, guaranteed.

Some of this art is absolute top drawer using design and printing techniques available nowhere else. Check the Resource section for a sampling of vendors.

EMBROIDERY:

Basic designs such as monograms can be sewn on fabric with a specially equipped household sewing machine. But make sure the sewing machine is attached to an experienced operator.

Creating sophisticated embroidered garments requires expensive, specialized equipment and lots of expertise—don't try this at home! If your project requires embroidery, shop around for price—even the low bid will be pricey, but there is no substitute for the high quality appearance of embroidery.

Much of the cost goes into preparing a tape. The tape is the roadmap that the special embroidery machine uses to sew your design. The rest of the cost is determined by the number of stitches and colors used. Be sure to have the embroiderer save your tape for future use.

Several vendors sell embroidered letters with a glue backing. These letters are pressed-on to a garment. If your project does not require art, such as a logo, this method will give you a good looking job at a small fraction of the cost of embroidering from scratch.

If you are interested in starting an embroidery business, check the resources for companies selling computer driven embroidery equipment. The capability of this equipment is awesome.

SCREENPRINTING:

To make screenprinting cost-effective you need to print several dozen shirts. Screenprinters have to charge you for making a screen for each color used in your design. Thus, spreading the screen cost over large quantities of shirts lowers the cost per shirt.

Screenprinter's capabilities vary from one shop to another. Shops with four color manual presses usually specialize in printing smaller quantities with one to four ink colors. A shop with an eight color automatic press is primarily interested in large runs with multiple colors.

For additional information see the Chapter 9.

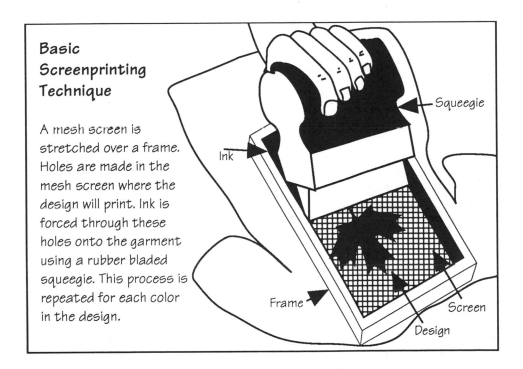

Basic Screenprinting Technique

A mesh screen is stretched over a frame. Holes are made in the mesh screen where the design will print. Ink is forced through these holes onto the garment using a rubber bladed squeegie. This process is repeated for each color in the design.

Squeegie

Ink

Frame

Screen

Design

GOCCO PRINTER

Think of this as miniaturized screenprinting equipment that you can take along on a picnic! The Gocco is sold as a kit inside a carrying case. Included is everything needed to print on cloth, paper, wood and even glass. Printing area is about 6" x 9". The company claims to have sold more than 7 million!

The Gocco is available from Gocco, 7526 Olympia View Drive, Suite E, Edmonds, Washington 98206 (1-800) 7781935.

TIE DYE:

As its name implies, shirts are tied in knots and dipped in fabric dye. Actually, you don't have to tie or dip. You can squirt, pour or paint the dye onto the shirt. Tie Dyeing is far more complex than any of the methods discussed above. If you are interested in trying this process call or write to Grateful Dyes in Colorado and ask for a copy of their catalog/instruction booklet.

They sell everything you'll need to make some very exotic designs. Check out their under $20 beginners dye kit. There is no doubt that these are one-of-a-kind shirts. Ask anybody who was around during the 1960's!

Tie Dyed shirts get their unique look from the various colored dyes into which they are dipped after first being tied together in some fashion.

"Tie Dye Color Cords" are a variation on the traditional tie process. The shirt is folded several times then tied with a cord. The cord contains the dyes which transfer to the shirt in an unstructured pattern making a unique tie-dye design. If you are doing only one shirt, this may be the ticket! Available from consolidated Thread Mills, Fall River, MA 02722.

Chapter 8

101 Things To Make With Transfers

Beyond designing custom T-shirts there lies numerous opportunities to apply your creative bent. The heat transfer method can be used on just about any fabric and a few other materials. The list below is not intended to be exhaustive, but rather to help stimulate your creativity and expand your possibilities. Take your pick and have fun!

BOXER SHORTS, UNDERGARMENTS

Its the new rage—your loved one's picture on your underwear? A little imagination along with the transfer technique will produce designer boxer shorts or other undergarments that will be talked about for years. In some families this is a must-have gift for valentines day. You'll need to lay out the design on the shorts before you heat press the transfer to avoid the bulky seams.

The transfer method can turn ordinary boxer shorts into designer shorts— sure to be a hit at bridal showers and other intimate gatherings.

You can heat press designs on other undergarments if this is your thing. Proceed cautiously with nylon fabric, practicing on scrap material if possible. See resources for vendors of these garments.

THE ANATOMY OF A T-SHIRT

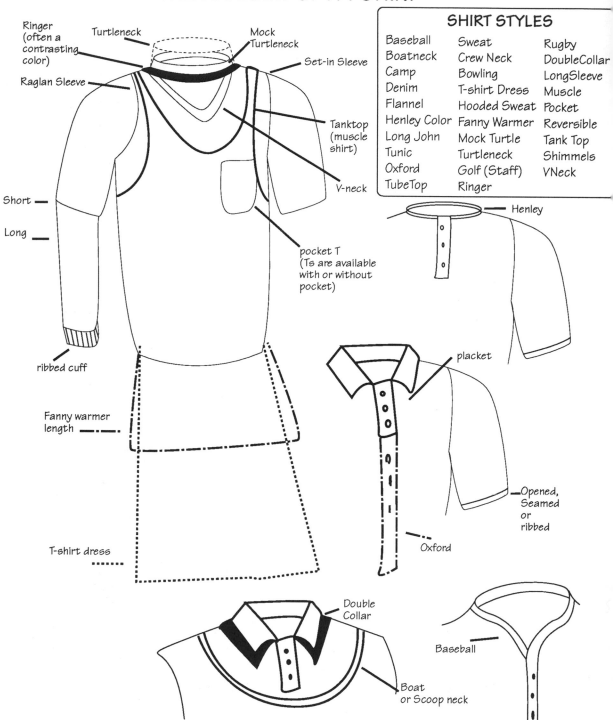

Ringer (often a contrasting color)

Turtleneck

Mock Turtleneck

Set-in Sleeve

Raglan Sleeve

Tanktop (muscle shirt)

V-neck

Short

Long

ribbed cuff

pocket T (Ts are available with or without pocket)

Fanny warmer length

T-shirt dress

SHIRT STYLES

Baseball	Sweat	Rugby
Boatneck	Crew Neck	DoubleCollar
Camp	Bowling	LongSleeve
Denim	T-shirt Dress	Muscle
Flannel	Hooded Sweat	Pocket
Henley Color	Fanny Warmer	Reversible
Long John	Mock Turtle	Tank Top
Tunic	Turtleneck	Shimmels
Oxford	Golf (Staff)	VNeck
TubeTop	Ringer	

Henley

placket

Opened, Seamed or ribbed

Oxford

Double Collar

Boat or Scoop neck

Baseball

SHIRTS:

The same methods used for T-shirts can be used on all shirt types. T-shirts and sweatshirts usually have a full size imprint on front or back or in both positions. If a heart patch design is used on the front, usually no other design area of the shirt is used.

Staff shirts nearly always have only a heart design (The design is about 3 1/2" wide and placed in the upper left hand heart position.) But there is no law prohibiting you from placing your design in other positions. Sleeves, tails, shoulders, even underarms can be used creatively.

FLAGS, BANNERS, WALLHANGINGS, CALENDARS

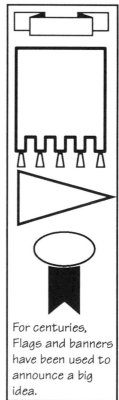

For centuries, Flags and banners have been used to announce a big idea.

A flag or banner is a welcome addition to a social or business event. A new baby, graduation, or surpassing sales goals seem to be more "real" with a flag or banner. If Hallmark sells a card about the day or event, a flag or banner is appropriate.

Surprise your friends or family who are celebrating something special by sending them a banner you design just for them—they will never forget it! Or how about designing an official flag for the Kingdom of Your Name, or a heraldic flag with your family crest (real or fabricated).

A quote or saying, decorative art, etc. printed on cloth and hung on a wall is called, appropriately, a wallhanging. But what is it when you hang a flag on a wall—a flag or a wallhanging? What are the rules for naming a piece of cloth a flag, a banner or a wallhanging? Since you are creating it you

A YEARLY CALENDAR

Print out a calendar that will last the whole year.

Not only is this a great family project, it also works great as a gift for customers, a fund raiser for organizations, or whenever you want to keep your message in the minds of the recipients.

After you heat press the fabric, wrap about an inch of the top around a stick such as a 1/4 inch dowel. Sew, glue or staple the edge to the back of the calendar. Attach string, ribbon, etc., to ends of stick.

For larger quantities, you can purchase ready-made calendars (with year and dates already printed) by the dozen from Comco, Inc, P.O.Box 9039, North Saint Paul, MN 55109, 1-800-328-9658.

The technique used in calendar making can also be used for creating wallhangings, pennants, flags, etc. For flags and pennants, use a larger stick (dowel) and, of course, make it in a horizontal configuration.

Or, attach the flag with grommets which are available in craft and many hardware stores.

A MONTHLY CALENDAR

Print out a calendar with a family member's picture inserted in their birthday month.

Mail a few to relatives, friends, distant family. Great Christmas or reunion gift idea.

Or have the kids make their own calendar art for Grandma using Draw-it, Wear-it transfers.

have the right to call it anything you want to call it.

A technique, called tiling, may be necessary if your design is large. Tiling is a special print feature of some computer programs. Essentially, the design is printed out onto transfer sheets, each sheet receiving only a small part of the design. These sheets are then assembled into a whole. Not unlike putting a puzzle together.

TILING

This method is used to create a large graphic which is too big for your printer to print in its entirety. The large graphic is divided into smaller segments. Each segment is printed individually and then "tiled"—the segments are put together to form the entire large graphic.

Would you believe—this method was used to cover the entire exterior of a five-story building!

This small segment of the whole graphic is put together with the other segments to form a large graphic. ▶

CAPS AND VISORS

Anything you can put on a T-shirt you can also print on the front panel of a cap (baseball hat), only smaller. A photo of your pet, a cultural statement, your company logo—whatever. Caps with white front panels work best when using the heat transfer method. You may have to spend some time jury rigging a rounded ironing board surface.

T-shirt shops use a cap press to embellish caps. This is a small heat press with a rounded ironing board that caps are slipped over and then heat pressed. Many T-shirt shops will press your caps for a small charge. Pressed-on

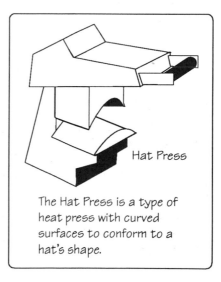

Hat Press

The Hat Press is a type of heat press with curved surfaces to conform to a hat's shape.

letters and the more expensive embroidery can be used to design your caps, especially if you are working with dark colored caps.

A unique item for caps is the pressed-on "scrambled eggs" which were originally used on hats of high-ranking military officers. Scrambled eggs are usually heat pressed on the visor of caps.

Scrambled Eggs! This 1/4" to 1/2" thick embroidered braiding has a glue backing allowing it to be heat pressed onto fabrics.

Cap Styles

Mesh	Paper	Gatsby	Visors
Poplin	Camouflage	Golf	Painters
Twill	Baseball	Panama	Knit
Wool	Cycling	Sailor	Denim
Metallic			Corduroy

TOTE BAGS, BACKPACKS, HIP PACKS

Totes are a great place to print that genuine or fictitious family crest. Like T-shirts, design ideas for totes are limitless—just about anything is appropriate. Imprinting totes and packs works best on white, natural or very light material. Warning: If you personalize a kids book bag, be prepared to handle the requests from the other kids in his or her class.

Bag Styles

Backpack
Duffle
Fanny
Garment
Sports
Laundry
Tote
Sports

Jones

Other styles of bags will work fine unless they are made of nylon or other synthetic material in which case be sure to use extreme caution in heat pressing as these materials scorch easily.

DOLLS

Picture a child's reaction when they receive a doll with *your* face on it. Or imagine the satisfaction of having your bosses face on a voodoo doll!

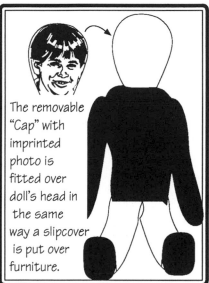

These are stuffed dolls about 15" tall with a removable cloth face on which you can print a heat transfer. The printed cloth is then slipped over the doll's head much like putting a slipcover over furniture. No matter how many of these you make you will never fail to be amused—they are a lot of fun.

The removable "Cap" with imprinted photo is fitted over doll's head in the same way a slipcover is put over furniture.

To get your picture on a doll "slipcover", transfer a photo onto the heat transfer sheet using a computer (see the section on *digitizing photos*) or copier (see *Copier Techniques* section) See *Resource* section for doll vendors.

As an alternative to a "store-bought" doll you can make your own in less than half an hour if you aren't looking for Barb/Ken quality. Heat press the face graphic onto an old T-Shirt or other fabric. Cut around the face in a large square, and sew it inside out like a pillow case (any sewing person can do this). Turn it inside out again and fill it with fabric scraps, socks, whatever. Use same process for arms, body, legs and stitch/staple them all together. Put on some yarn for hair, maybe a doll's dress, socks whatever you have.

TOWELS, BIBS AND DIAPERS

Diapers with an imprint? Why not?

Bibs and kitchen tea towels can also be imprinted as long as they do not have a long fiber nap.

Any fabric with a long nap cannot be heat pressed satisfactorily. The long fibers on terry cloth have to be saturated with ink, and a transfer does not have enough ink to saturate these fibers. Not even the screenprinting method is able to print on this material without special equipment. If you need terry cloth fabric printed, see the *Resource* section for screenprinters who specialize in this area.

PILLOWCASES, BEDSHEETS

If you have ever been awakened from a nightmare not knowing where you were, here's the solution. On a white pillowcase heat press the words "you are here". From the erotic to the sublime, pillowcase designs are limitless. They make great gag gifts.

Bedsheets require a few more heat transfers than pillow cases, but the thought of owning a custom designed (designer) bed sheet is too much for many to resist. And what a gift idea!

Children love bedsheets that are imprinted with their names-the more and bigger the names the better. Here's a low-tech idea for kids sheets that they will absolutely love. Using fabric magic markers or fabric paint let them design their own bedsheet. Another fun idea is to have all their friends or school-mates sign the bedsheet—even teenagers like this one.

If you have teens living in your house you may have to contain their zeal when they discover they can print their girlfriend's/boyfriend's picture on their pillowcase or photos of their 26 absolute, most favorite musical groups on the bedsheets.

Whenever you design a bedsheet, be sure to sign your work and point out to everyone that you have designer sheets (you are the designer, aren't you?)

HANDKERCHIEFS, SCARFS, BANDANAS, TIES

Blowing your nose on a picture of your sibling, wearing a scarf designed by your first grader—these are a few of the many possibilities.

Ties can be cut from fabric, printed and then folded into a tie. Or, unfold a ready made tie, heat press and refold. Use standard heat-press techniques unless the fabric is silk, nylon or satin, in which case you'll need a few test runs before final print. These fabrics scorch easily.

QUILTS

Sweet dreams are guaranteed when you sleep with your whole family. Pull out the family album and heat press all their pictures onto four to six inch pieces of cloth (patches). To get the photos onto the patches see the sections on *Digitizing photos* or *Copier Techniques*. Make a few more patches with uncle Willy's wise sayings or tidbits of family history. Take all these patches and sew them together to form a large sheet of patches. Sew this to the back of a bedsheet or other fabric and you have an irre-placeable heirloom. Unless you have experience with quilts you might want to read one of the many books on the subject at your local library. Remember, this is a family heirloom. If you don't know how to sew, enlist a family member. After all, what are families for?

Your local library or craft store will have books on quilting. One book to look for is Designing Your Own Quilts *by William Soltow*

APRONS, JACKETS, SMOCKS

Studies show that men will gladly wear a designed apron outdoors (near a barbecue) but not in the kitchen. Women will wear an apron in the kitchen but not outside the house!

Smocks—if you design one of these for men, call it a lab coat. For a woman, call it the latest fashion rage.

Use the T-shirt heat transfer tech-niques to embellish aprons, lab coats, artist smocks, jackets—unless they are made of satin or nylon. These fabrics scorch easily and require a practice run before doing the final print.

Aprons can be purchased ready for your design or cut out of nearly any fabric. Ribbon, shoelaces or string can be used as ties.

HAND PUPPETS

Two pieces of cloth sewn together, turned inside out and decorated with face/body art = hand puppet!

Print an actual photograph of a child's imaginative friend on the doll's face and you have a therapy doll. Or how about a photo puppet of each employee in the office—if the puppet speaks the real thoughts of the employee can he/she be fired? After all, the puppet, not the employee, said it didn't he/she/it?

Hand puppets are easy to make. Printing a person's photo on the doll's face makes this doll into an alter ego—or maybe just a lot of fun.

CLOTH BOOKS FOR TODDLERS

Personalizing a book for toddlers will be a big hit with parents and grandparents, especially if the book features photos and stories centered around the family members. Imagine how the toddler will treasure this book when they become adults. Be sure to make an extra copy for out-of-town relatives.

Don't allow a lack of drawing skills stop you from making one of these books. Neither the artistic quality nor the story line will matter very much. A photo of child's head placed on a stick figure will mean more to the child than a professionally rendered illustration done by a stranger.

If your book has multiple pages which must be bound together, your best approach is to print a double-sided page, bind the pages together and then trim the edges. Trimming the pages before binding tends to make the edges look a bit ragged.

To end up with an eight page book with each page measuring 8 1/2" x 11", for example, print on both sides of two 11" x 17" sheets, After binding these two sheets together and folding, you have an eight page book.. This methods works for any size book. Plan the page layout before you begin, as your pages will be numbered according to how they fit together after binding. (see illustration)

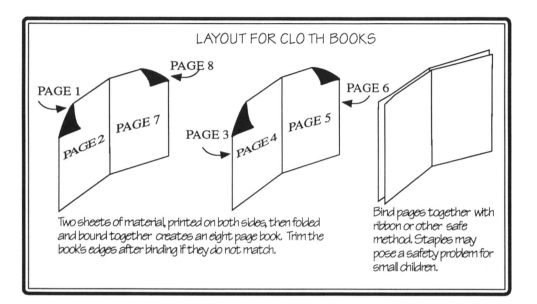

LAYOUT FOR CLOTH BOOKS

Two sheets of material, printed on both sides, then folded and bound together creates an eight page book. Trim the book's edges after binding if they do not match.

Bind pages together with ribbon or other safe method. Staples may pose a safety problem for small children.

TENNIS SHOES

Why not emblazon your own name on your tennis shoes instead of paying big bucks to wear a sport figure's name.

The heat transfer and other methods can be used on canvas tennis shoes. The trick here is to design a hard surface that fits into the shoe. Practicing on scrap material is advised. If you get serious about this technique, Geo Knight company (1-800-525-6766) sells a machine that prints tennis shoes.

PET APPAREL

The inhabitants of tropical fish tanks and ant farms are hard to fit with customized pet apparel, but just about any other pet qualifies. Ready made or home made apparel embellished with the pet's name or slogan will make your pet the envy of the neighborhood animal kingdom. Add a few drawings of flower or other decorative art and you have a one-of-a-kind conversation piece.

Choose a fabric that readily receives a transfer imprint. Knits and naps are difficult if not impossible to imprint.

If your pet is sensitive about wearing flashy duds, there is always an alternative way to show your pets how special they are: a flag for a doghouse, a custom designed kitty cushion, custom printed leashes and collars, a photo wallhanging of your pet pig hung on the living room wall.

WEATHERPROOF MAPS

The photo footage shows police officers, fire fighters and boy scouts combing the area searching for a lost soul in the great and sometimes hostile outdoors. Lost and starving because their paper map disintegrated in the rain.

Hikers, bikers, campers, hunters–any outdoor enthusiast-will never again have to worry about getting lost when you design a weather proof map for their next big outing.

Maps can be drawn by hand on Draw-it Wear-it transfers and heat pressed onto a naturally stiff fabric such as light canvas. Other fabrics will work as well, but outdoors people seem to like the rugged look and feel of canvas.

With drawing software, using the heat transfer method, you can computer design a map that would rival a Rand-McNally version. The copier technique may also be used.

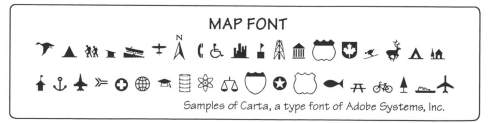

MAP FONT

Samples of Carta, a type font of Adobe Systems, Inc.

If you plan to do several maps you may want to consider buying a special map font. Adobe, for example, sells a map font they call Carta. This font includes Just about every symbol used on conventional maps.

BUTTONS AND BADGES

To make a few buttons and badges, find an old button and cover it with the graphic you print on cloth. The width of the button is your printing area. Add a half inch around the button width, cut out this cloth print and wrap it around the button, gluing the cloth edges to the button back.

Heat transfer printing an occasional button, badge or bumper sticker is an easy matter. Printing a lot of these may not be worth the trouble as it is much easier, faster and cheaper to have these done by vendors or to do it yourself with the inexpensive specialized equipment designed for this type of work.

If you plan to make buttons frequently or in large quantities you can get an inexpensive button maker press from Badge-A-Minit (See *resources*)

Decals which can be viewed through glass such as those used on car rear windows can be made by printing the graphic on acetate material (a transparency sheet designed specifically for your printer—see resources) Print the graphic "mirrored". Spray glue on the non-printed side and place the decal onto the glass, rubbing it to get a tight bond.
A removable spray glue such as 3M Spray Mount works best.

BUMPER STICKERS

A few bumper stickers can be made using the transfer method by simply printing out the message on appropriate fabric and gluing it onto the bumper. While there is not doubt that cloth bumper stickers would be a novelty, printing a large number of these could become expensive. You may find it easier and cheaper to print these out on a sheet of paper which you can then duplicate on a copier and then have them laminated at an office supply store or other vendor who provides this service.

If bumper stickers are your thing, write or call one of the companies listed in *Resources* that sells bumper stickers or bumper sticker making equipment.

WINDSOCKS

Here is a scientific method to demonstrate that your relative or friend is full of hot air—hold up your windsock when they talk.

You can heat transfer onto a ready made sock, but it is tricky. Its a lot easier to make your own windsock from any available fabric, heat press your graphic and then sew or glue the whole thing together.

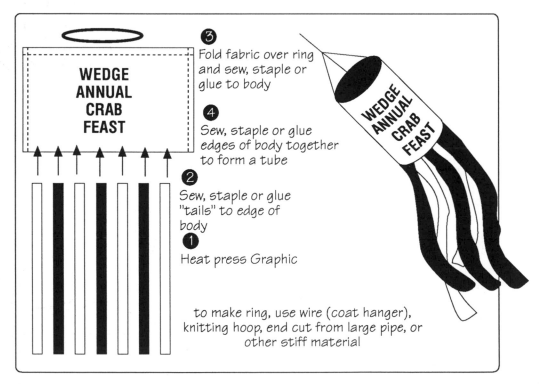

WEDGE ANNUAL CRAB FEAST

③ Fold fabric over ring and sew, staple or glue to body

④ Sew, staple or glue edges of body together to form a tube

② Sew, staple or glue "tails" to edge of body

① Heat press Graphic

to make ring, use wire (coat hanger), knitting hoop, end cut from large pipe, or other stiff material

DID WE MENTION!

Director's/Beach Chairs
Drink Coasters
Key chains
Wallets
Puzzles
Placemats
Suspenders
Napkins
Book Markers
Gift wrap
Gift wrap ribbon
Potholders
Book Covers
Auto Sun Shades
Christmas Ornament
Vests
Bags (Sacks)
Headbands
Wristbands
Pajamas
Golf Club Covers
Gloves
Table Clothes/Runners
Umbrellas
Mousepads
Car shades
Slipcovers
Shoelaces
Kites
Shower Curtains
Blue Ribbons
Christmas Stocking
Posters
Doillies

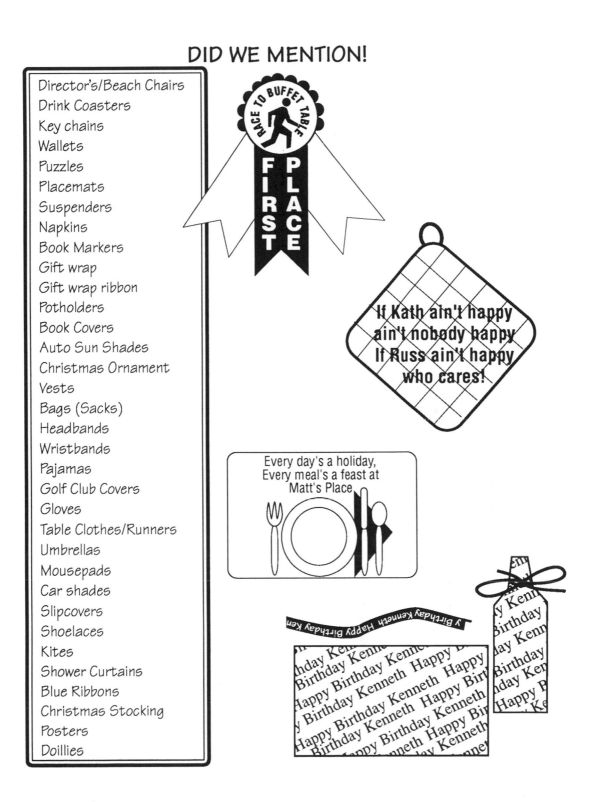

RACE TO BUFFET TABLE

FIRST PLACE

If Kath ain't happy ain't nobody happy If Russ ain't happy who cares!

Every day's a holiday, Every meal's a feast at Matt's Place

Happy Birthday Kenneth

BOOK JACKET (COVER)

Jacket Outside

COVER DESIGN

COVER DESIGN

Jacket Inside

Cover of book slips into pockets

JANE
LOVES
TO
READ
&
READS
OF
LOVE

Xavier
holds
the key
to my
heart

Dear Brian

GO FLY A
KITE

Sally

★Skippy★

MARY

Chapter 9

Computer Screenprinting Process

Screenprinting T-shirts can be both an art form and a serious business. As an art form it is used to produce original art with results that are hard, if not impossible, to duplicate by any other media. As a business it can be exciting and highly profitable.

The T-Shirt has become a part of the American (and world) culture. It is virtually impossible to go into a public area where screenprinted T-Shirts are not worn. Screenprinting is a huge business and is growing by leaps and bounds.

Large corporations produce the millions of T's that are sold in national chain stores. But the shirts worn by local teams and groups are produced by local T-shirt makers—in small T-shirt factories, T-shirt shops, private garages and basements.

THE SCREENPRINTING PROCESS

Here's an easy way to understand the screenprinting process. Using a screen door, we coat the screen with something like glue or shellac so the holes in the screen are covered over (closed). Using a pin, poke out the glue/shellac in several places—lots of holes, maybe in the shape of your name. Put some ink on the screen and push it against the screen. The ink will go only through the holes you made. If you held the screen against a fabric, you will see your name printed.

The function of the wood frame of the screen door is the same as that in the screenprinting process—the stretched screen is held in place. In screenprinting, the "screen" is actually a coated mesh material. Instead of making a design by poking holes in the screen, a special camera "burns" the image into the screen—removing the coating on the screen where the design is to be printed. The ink is forced through the image area on the screen by pushing the ink through using a "squeegee"—a tool similar to the rubber-bladed tool used for cleaning windows.

This process is repeated for each color in the design. The screen is then mounted onto a screenprinting press. A good press will align all the screens so that the colors "register" in the right place. The garment is placed on the press and the first color screen is placed on the shirt. Ink is put on the screen surface and pulled lengthwise over the screen with a squeegee. This forces the ink through the design's open mesh area onto the garment. The garment now has the first color imprinted on it. The press is rotated to bring the second color in position over the garment. This process is repeated for all other colors.

Ink takes time to dry so very rapid drying is necessary to prevent the ink from smearing the shirt and from sticking to the back of the second screen. A special flash dryer is used for this purpose.

The entire screenprinting process is rather simple to perform as long as you use the right equipment and high-quality supplies—particularly the screens and ink.

Who Buys Screenprinted Garments?

Teams
Clubs
Organizations
Causes
Individuals
Events
Companies
Schools
Colleges
Fraternities
Sororities
Politicals
Churches
Non-Profits
Entreprenuers
Promotors
Fund Raisers
Ad Specialists

SCREENPRINTING EQUIPMENT

Special equipment must be used to make the screens, to print and to dry the shirt. The array of equipment being sold today is mind boggling. Buying the right equipment can make the difference in success or failure in a start-up venture. The best bet is to buy only the basics from a reputable dealer and build from there as your business volume demands. A lot of people want to sell you stuff you really don't need at start-up, or ever for that matter.

Most screenprinters start small, often in their basement or garage, buying a manually operated four color press, a few screens, some ink and a portable dryer. Several vendors specialize in this start-up type equipment. If you decide to purchase equipment check out the reputation of the vendor. There are a few fly-by night outfits around. Being stuck with inferior, over-priced equipment that can't be repaired or upgraded could be devastating to a new business.

A few vendors sell equipment packages that include everything you would need to start a moonlighting or full-time screenprinting business. Buying a screenprinting package avoids making mistakes in mismatched equipment, and the cost is usually lower than purchasing the items separately. Package vendors are also a helpful source during start-up—often offering advice, technical support and reputable sources of supplies.

SCREENPRINTING FOR PROFIT

Handsome profits are to be made in this business. According to Entrepreneur Magazine, local T-Shirt shops with this type of equipment earn $35,000 to $200,000 a year. Experts agree that it is wise to start small and grow big instead of jumping into a large overhead operation. Like anything else in life, time and experience will hone your screenprinting skills and give you a better idea of which market niche you enjoy working in. As the saying goes, if you do what you enjoy, the money will follow. And in the screenprinting industry, this can be a big following!

Combining conventional screenprinting with computer generated T-shirts is a good move for serving customers who, it has been predicted, will demand customized products, when they want it, and at a good price-quality ratio. To keep prices low and profit high avoid getting caught up in the newest and latest—stay with the low overhead basic equipment until its impossible not to upgrade.

Full-time shops serving a larger area eventually have to trade up to a multiple color, often automatic press so they can produce a larger volume and not be forced to turn away high volume eight color business.

If you have an interest in entering this field, get a subscription to a few of the magazines and books listed in the *resource* section.

COMPUTER PREPARATION

You can save some money and keep control of your design by preparing the artwork for the screenprinter. If your design uses only one color, make a black and white printout. The screenprinter can then put this into his camera and blow it up to the size he needs. He will use the negative made from his camera to burn your design onto a silkscreen. Ask your screenprinter if his equipment can handle screens (percentages of a color) or gradations if any are included in your design. These gradated screens are often a no no.

For graphics with more than one color you will need to prepare a color separation. Print color separations from your computer if you have a graphics program and a laser printer. If you have never done this, check it out in your graphic software manual. It is a simple process but the actual method differs from one software program to another.

If your graphics program does not have a separation capability, simply print out each color separately. For example: let's say your design uses red and blue; temporarily delete the blue parts and print out only the red. Vice versa for the blue parts. Each color will, of course, print out black—that's the only color the screenprinter's camera will work with. The color on the shirt's design is determined by the color of the ink used.

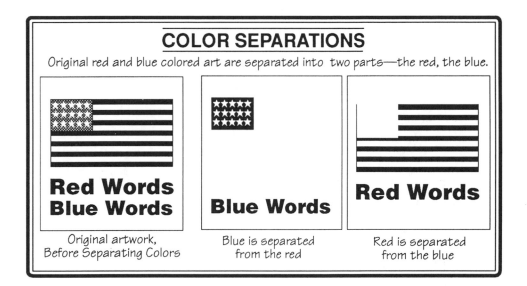

Photographs and Screenprinting

Screenprinting a photograph requires a screenprinting press that can print *process* colors. But first, the photo must be color separated by a company specializing in this type of work. The cost of a photo color separation starts at $400. Separation shops are listed in the *Resource* section,

Process printing uses four ink colors, blue (cyan), red (magenta), yellow and black. These are referred to as CMYK. These four colors and combined with various percentages of each color to create any color of the rainbow. You may be familiar with this if you have ever combined yellow and blue dyes to get a green color when coloring eggs or in watercoloring.

While you can make a process color separation in a photo manipulation program such as Corel Draw, you should first check with the screenprinter to determine how he needs the seps prepared. This may become complicated, requiring trapping, etc., But if you know how to use the software you should have little difficulty separating the photo.

If the cost of photo separation is prohibitive, consider using a line art version of the photo. (See this technique on page 66) This method will require only one color for the line art, making a much cheaper screen print.

CUSTOMIZING SCREEN PRINTED GARMENTS

There are a number of ways to personalize screen printed garments with the transfer method. If your design is on the back of a shirt, each member of a bowling team can have his/her name on the front. For sports teams, shirts with a design on the front can be customized with team member's numbers on the back.

Customizing within a screenprinted graphic is also possible if certain precautions are taken. To avoid removing part of the already printed area, protect the area by covering it with a piece of cloth before heat pressing the custom transfer.

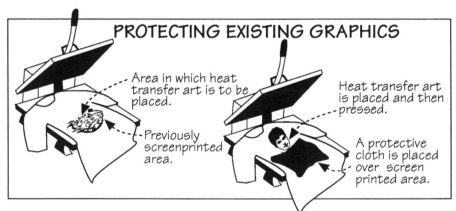

PROTECTING EXISTING GRAPHICS

Area in which heat transfer art is to be placed.

Previously screenprinted area.

Heat transfer art is placed and then pressed.

A protective cloth is placed over screen printed area.

A similar technique should be used with hand iron.

Chapter 10

T-Shirts
For
Profit

If you already own computer equipment why not use it to make T-shirts for profit. Make extra money selling T-shirts to your family, friends and coworkers plus any teams and groups with which you are associated. You will be amazed how many people buy designed T-shirts and how easy it is to make a nice profit.

Customers may have to be educated on the fact that custom-designed shirts, as is the case in anything customized, cost more than the mass produced variety. Twenty to twenty-five dollars a shirt is not extreme. Of course, you'll sell more at $15 each.

Set a price for designs you create and another price for designs the customer creates. And don't forget to charge for both front and back printing–your costs and time will double and your price has to reflect this.

Should you decide to invest more time, you can increase your sales by letting various businesses, teams and organizations know you are available to do custom T's. The benefits to stress to your potential clients are those services that screenprinters can't offer: the custom aspect of your shirts; no minimum order; photos; and no limit or extra cost for colors (if you have a color printer).

MOONLIGHT MADNESS

Because your product and service are above average (and average is incredibly average), members of the groups initially contacted will spread the word. In a short time you will have more work than you can handle.

This is decision time. Continuing to take more orders than you can easily produce will soon show up in your product quality or your service. Compromising on quality or service will put you into the "average" class where there is a lot of competition and not much money. To keep your reputation and your profits you will need to made one of two choices: cut back on clients, encouraging only those you enjoy working with, or devote more time to your booming business.

SPECIALIZING YOUR BUSINESS

Now that this is becoming a serious business you may want to focus on niche markets. Trying to be everything to everybody is a tough way to run a business. Your expertise, equipment and supplies will need to have a very wide range of application, Unless you are well funded, this all things to all people will prove difficult if not impossible to maintain. Generalists are vulnerable to any competitor who is bigger or better financed. Its a case of being a little fish in a big pond or a big fish in a small pond. In a niche market you can be the big fish—respected, in demand and never going hungry.

Some niche markets are so large, pets for example, that one person can't handle all the work. You may have to find a niche within a niche to keep the market manageable. How far to "niche down" is determined by your available time, expertise and interest.

An example of Niche Down levels: 1 pets, 2 dogs, 3 dalmations, 4 pedigreed dalmations, 5 pedigreed dalmations, owned by national club members. No matter which market you choose, you'll soon be known as an expert in that field. Experts get more and better paying work.

Finding Customers in a Niche Market

"The way to catch a fish is to think like a fish" and to think like a fish focus your attention on the things that fish do. What periodicals do they read, to what organizations do they belong. Read the same stuff, join the same groups. In short order, you will think like a fish.

Any librarian can show you the reference book that will identify the groups, periodicals, books, etc. that relate to your fish. There is no niche, no matter how obscure, that can escape the prowess of a good librarian—none.

GOING ON THE ROAD

If you don't get excited about the long hours and other demands of retail, or aren't thrilled about being confined to a home office, then take your show on the road. The opportunities are literally unlimited.

Just about any type of gathering has potential for profit. Some custom T-shirt makers are earning very good livings specializing in this mobile business—selling their shirts to small and large groups, from bar mitzvahs to state fairs,

Private gatherings such as a graduation party, require you to negotiate an agreement with the host or committee. The arrangement can be as simple as agreeing upon the price at which the shirt is sold. Some groups are happy just to have you come in and offer the service to make their affair more exciting.

Other groups, particularly charitable organizations, will require you to give a percentage of shirt sales to the charity. Quite often, they will provide you with a volunteer to help you make the shirts or whatever other help you may need. (If you agree to this arrangement, be sure to make a big sign telling the participants that you are contributing to the charity—it will increase your sales substantially.)

Still another common arrangement for private groups is a package purchase. The host signs an agreement with you to purchase a set number of shirts, usually at a discounted price. She is purchasing the shirts for every invited guest. You simply crank out the shirts as requested by the guests.

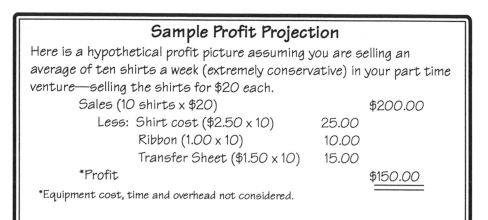

Sample Profit Projection

Here is a hypothetical profit picture assuming you are selling an average of ten shirts a week (extremely conservative) in your part time venture—selling the shirts for $20 each.

Sales (10 shirts x $20)		$200.00
Less: Shirt cost ($2.50 x 10)	25.00	
Ribbon (1.00 x 10)	10.00	
Transfer Sheet ($1.50 x 10)	15.00	
*Profit		$150.00

*Equipment cost, time and overhead not considered.

A Real World Example

A firefighter, in her off-duty time, designs T-shirts for fellow firefighters in her district and surrounding jurisdictions. She averages 26 shirts per week. Much of this work is obtained by word of mouth, while the remainder comes from renting a booth at the annual county and state fire conventions. She has no advertising budget, no storefront rent, no overhead whatsoever. Last year she netted over $19,000 in her part time venture, working an average of eleven hours a week!

This is a perfect business for her—she can work when she wants (an important issue for a swingshift firefighter) and she deals only with a subject she understands and enjoys.

Public gatherings, such as fairs and conventions, are great places to make a very good profit. This can be a full time business if travel is not a problem for you. Some estimate there are 7,000 fairs/conventions every day of the year. Your librarian can point you in the direction of reference books which list every convention going on anywhere at anytime.

The downside of the mobile T-shirt maker is lugging the equipment around—a computer, printer, heat press and camcorder. A van works nice for this, but you can also get it all in a compact car. Granted, it takes a little more ingenuity. Some mobile folks use a cart on which they roll the equipment to the display area.

Using the area provided by clients, conventions, fairs, etc. helps keep down your luggage. But if you will be working in an outdoor activity such as a flea market, you will have to take along a tarpaulin or other waterproof arrangements to protect your equipment against rain, etc.,

The big profits in selling to both private and public groups is in the customizing of T-shirts. People are thrilled to have a shirt designed the way *they* want it. When one person buys a shirt you will soon see others lining up for theirs. You can promote this by displaying sample shirts and having your computer screen visible to the audience.

If possible, relate your shirts to the subject of the activity. The impulse inertia is already built into the customer by the atmosphere created by the affair. A theme connection will more than double your sales.

PROTOTYPING

One type of work you may wish to add to your repertory is prototyping. Prototyping a T-shirt is like making a model of the real thing—in this case, the real thing is a large volume run of a screenprinted shirt. Graphic design firms, ad agencies, specialty ad and even silk screeners need to first sell their client on a shirt concept before printing hundreds or thousands of shirts. The computer transfer system or a big bank roll are the only ways to prototype.

Most of these clients prepare their own artwork, you simply print it out of your computer. Ask the client to supply the design on computer disk. Otherwise you will need to scan the art into your computer. Either way, this is a very profitable niche.
If you live in a metropolitan area, you could earn a good living doing prototyping exclusively.

This type of business can be operated from your home if you wish. People in the graphics/advertising business have only one mode of operation—rush. Being able to meet their "needed it three days ago" demand will make you indispensable no matter where your business is housed. And they don't even blink when you invoice them at $45 a shirt!

LET THEIR FINGERS DO THE WALKING

Your business will really take off when you put an ad in the yellow pages. Before you take this giant step, make sure you have the time and expertise to produce an enormous variety of customer orders—everything and anything you can imagine a T-shirt design to be will be demanded of you. From the ridiculous to the truly bizarre will be your everyday requests. No matter how jaded or worldly you think you are, you will be constantly amazed at how strange and creative peoples ideas can be.

You will have to turn down a lot of work from yellow page customers if you don't also screenprint. Starting your own screenprinting shop is pretty serious business. If you are interested in entering this field, helpful guidance is available from the associations and magazines listed in the appendix.

Making Yellow Page Ads Work Hard

Make a profile of the customer you want to attract. Focus every word of the ad to that hypothetical customer. Stress only the benefits the customer gets by purchasing your product. Customers aren't interested in you or your needs. They only want to know what you can do for them and how long it will take. Keep it as simple as possible.

Yellow Page ads are a quick read—break through the clutter with a design like you use on a T-shirt, tell the story in a five second read.

A company name can tell a lot about your service. For example, T-Shirt Genius says a lot more than F.J.Z. Enterprises.

Don't assume other ads are good because they are big. Most of them are not. They often bring in less money than they cost! A well done small to medium size add will outpull a poorly done large ad anytime.

BROKERING

The alternative to becoming a screenprinter is brokering. With a little research you can find several good screenprinters in your area who will give you wholesale prices.

You take the customer's shirt order, farm it out to your screenprinters and collect the profit margin between the wholesale and retail price. Why would you farm out work instead of doing it yourself on the computer? You farm work out when it saves you time or money, or you just can't do what the client wants.

Time: The computer method is by far the fastest way to do shirts, *unless* the quantity is large. Once a screenprinter has his equipment setup he can produce large volumes of shirts very rapidly.

Money: The screenprinter's cost to produce large volumes of shirts is low—even lower than your computer generating costs—because his costs after setup are merely ink, the shirts and very little labor. When you spread the setup cost over hundreds of shirts it makes screenprinting very cost effective.

You can't do it: Your costs and time to produce a black or dark colored shirt are higher than a white or light-colored shirt. Opaquing requires you to use extra materials and an additional pressing step. Screenprinters can print light ink on dark shirts without extra cost or effort. Unless you are printing less than a dozen black or dark shirts, it is wiser to use a screenprinter. The same applies to exotic client demands such as glow-in-the-dark ink, metallic ink, three-dimensional ink. (Of course, if only lettering is involved you can do all of these exotics with pressed-on lettering)

Brokering is a service business. Give outstanding service to your customers and you can't help but succeed. Specializing in a niche, such as sport uniforms, can make you the sought after guru. Brokering can be a very lucrative business with little up-front costs.

The Secret Service

The secret to this business is service–back-bending, go-the extra-mile service. With this kind of operation you will grow very fast—that kind of service is one of the rarest commodities in the real world.

To test out this service theory for yourself, call a few randomly selected screenprinters from your phone book and ask them for a price and turnaround time on a dozen, three color shirts. Listen carefully to their attitude and you be the judge!

LEARNING THE BUSINESS OF BUSINESS

In recent years small businesses have become big business. Your local library or bookstore is stocked full with all sorts of information on starting and operating a small business. There are literally hundreds of book titles on the subject. Reading one or two of these books may help you get your business off to the right start or get it booming sooner than you thought possible.

Pay particular attention to information on accounting and marketing. The failure of most businesses can usually be traced to a failure in one or both of these areas. You can have the world's best service or product and still fail to succeed in business. The world does not beat a path to your door—you have to beat a path to their door! Businesses that have good accounting and marketing systems are rarely forced out of business—even if their product and service is mediocre. Imagine what your outstanding products and service could accomplish.

The best help you can get in the T-shirt business is from people in the T-shirt business. The magazines, books and associations listed in the appendix will guide you in finding the best sources of information in any area of the garment industry. There is a wealth of information available, usually just for the asking.

Heard recently from an employee of a national service company:
"We provide quality, service and price—pick two!"

Chapter 11

Coffee
Mugs
Etc.

This chapter has absolutely nothing to do with T-Shirts—well, almost nothing. Soon after you master the T-shirt technique you'll probably be wondering what other wild and crazy things you can do with your computer. So here are a few things you can make to justify all the money you spent on that computer.

CERAMIC COFFEE MUGS

Commercial mugs are most often decorated using ceramic paint or screenprinting techniques. Neither of these methods is feasible for customized short-run quantities.

Dye sublimation is the method of choice to create custom designed ceramic or ironstone mugs. The imprinted design is

---

Printing With Dye Sublimation

Dot-Matrix Printer	Use special dye-sub ribbon
Laser Printer	Use special dye-sub toner cartridge
Wax Thermal Printer	Not applicable
Ink Jet	Use special dye-sub cartridge
Dye Sub Printer	Use regular ribbon
Vidoe Printer	Use regular ribbon

dishwasher safe and will last indefinitely.

Computer Method:

Photos, text, art—anything you can get into your computer—can be printed on a mug with the dye sub method. The quality of the imprint is excellent, the colors vivid.

Simply print your design onto dye-sub paper using a template of approximately 3" x 8" (To measure the exact printable area of a mug, first wrap a sheet of paper around mug starting at the edge of handle, pencil mark where paper ends and then measure the paper length). Place graphics near ends of the template to create a design on both sides of mug. Wrap a 3" x 8" sheet of paper around the mug marking the position where you want the design to print. Use this sheet as your template.

For a wraparound design, place graphic on entire template from end to end.

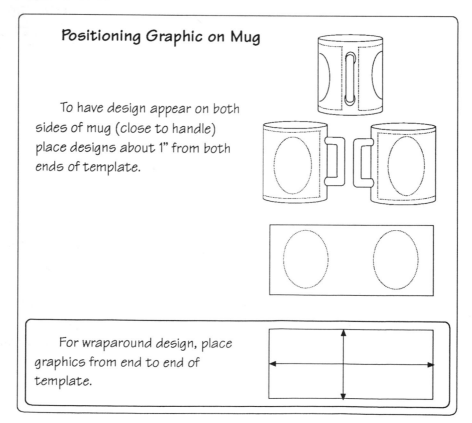

Positioning Graphic on Mug

To have design appear on both sides of mug (close to handle) place designs about 1" from both ends of template.

For wraparound design, place graphics from end to end of template.

Video Printer:

A video printer can also be used to create mug designs. This type of printer prints a small (about 3" x 5") dye sublimation. Some models are capable of printing text, but for the most part, they are used to print photographs captured from an input device such as a video camera, VCR, etc. Sharp, Cannon and others manufacture these printers. Their price ranges from $500 up. The QLT company specializes in these printers and carries a huge supply of film, etc..

Transferring design:

Transferring the design to the mug is the same with either the computer or video method of dye-sublimation printing. The printed paper is wrapped around the mug, taped in position, and placed into a mug press.

Like T-shirts, heat and pressure are applied to bond the graphic onto the surface of the mug. This surface is specially coated on the outside to receive dye-sub prints. Mugs purchased from vendors listed in the resource section all sell coated mugs.

If you wish to use a non-coated mug, or print on the handle or inside bottom, you will need to first coat the mug yourself. Instant T's Company (800) 221-9041 sells a mug-coating kit for this purpose.

Mug Press:

A mug press is the simplest, fastest way to heat-press a graphic onto a mug. The mug, with graphic paper taped on, is placed in the press. The handle is pulled down and the press heats the mug under the right amount of pressure to the length of time set by you. (See illustration below)

These presses sell new for $500 up. For occasional use, have a press owner press your mug. Mug press owners, like T-shirt heat press owners, can be found in various places (See list in Nitty Gritty chapter)

Oven Bake:

Designs can be baked onto mugs in ovens and micro-waves. To create the necessary pressure, mugs are wrapped in special pressure jigs. (See illustration, facing page) This method is also capable to heat pressing mug handles, inside bottoms and various sized plates.

PLASTIC COFFEE MUGS:

No special equipment is needed to create the plastic mug. Since the medium used is paper, Just about any computer or non-computer method can be used to design plastic mugs.

First, the mug's inside liner is removed. A strip of paper is designed, inserted between the clear outside plastic and the inside white plastic liner. The inside liner is then replaced.

These plastic mugs are dishwasher safe and long lasting. Because the paper artwork is sandwiched between two pieces of plastic it isn't affected by dish washing, dirty hands, etc.

The QLT company is a source for these mugs. They also sell pre-designed paper strips.

Plastic Snap-In Mug Technique

1 Print a design on paper or cloth and cut into a strip about 3" by 8"

2 Remove white plastic insert from mug.

3 Place the designed strip into mug, design side facing out.

4 Replace the white plastic insert into the mug.

Techniques For Printing Ceramic Coffee Mugs

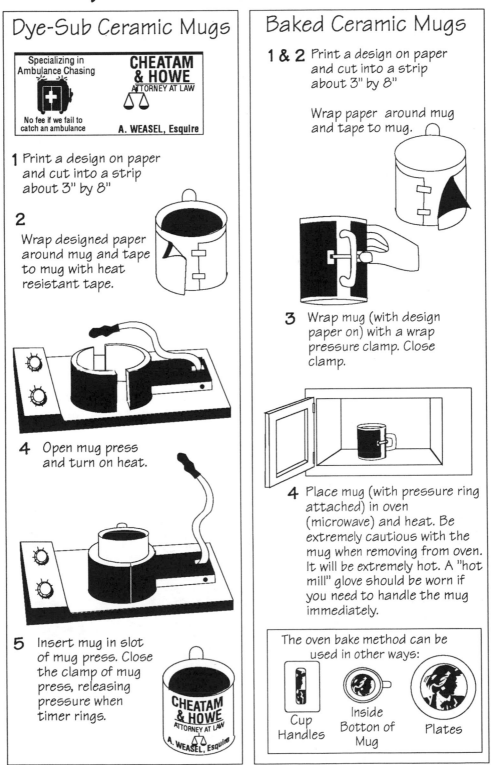

Dye-Sub Ceramic Mugs

Specializing in Ambulance Chasing

CHEATAM & HOWE
ATTORNEY AT LAW

No fee if we fail to catch an ambulance

A. WEASEL, Esquire

1 Print a design on paper and cut into a strip about 3" by 8"

2 Wrap designed paper around mug and tape to mug with heat resistant tape.

4 Open mug press and turn on heat.

5 Insert mug in slot of mug press. Close the clamp of mug press, releasing pressure when timer rings.

CHEATAM & HOWE
ATTORNEY AT LAW
A. WEASEL, Esquire

Baked Ceramic Mugs

1 & 2 Print a design on paper and cut into a strip about 3" by 8"

Wrap paper around mug and tape to mug.

3 Wrap mug (with design paper on) with a wrap pressure clamp. Close clamp.

4 Place mug (with pressure ring attached) in oven (microwave) and heat. Be extremely cautious with the mug when removing from oven. It will be extremely hot. A "hot mill" glove should be worn if you need to handle the mug immediately.

The oven bake method can be used in other ways:

Cup Handles

Inside Bottom of Mug

Plates

PRINTING ON METAL

Dye sublimation can also be used on a number of other materials, including metal. After printing out a graphic (can include photos) it is heat pressed onto a flat metal surface in much the same way a T-shirt is heat pressed. The metallic luster adds a new dimension to whatever you print on the metal plate. It gives a subtle glow and an iridescence to the design.

Metal plates are available in several finishes, but primarily in silver and burnished gold. Adding a printed border or gluing the metal plate to a wooden plaque gives an entirely different look to the piece. Vendors have all sorts of sizes, styles, embellishments available.

Dye sublimation printers or computer printers with dye-sub ribbon/cartridge capability are capable of printing for this metal technique. (See printer-type list at beginning of chapter)

SNAP-INS

These items are created in much the same way as the plastic mug discussed above. A designed piece of paper is sandwiched between two surfaces, usually plastic. This sandwich is configured in different ways to create novelty items.

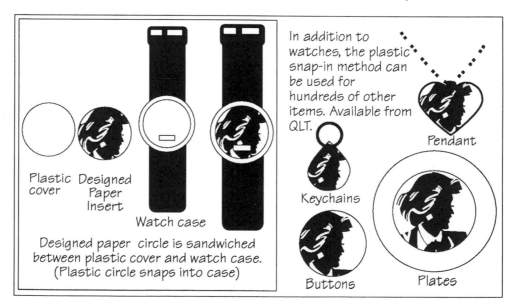

In addition to watches, the plastic snap-in method can be used for hundreds of other items. Available from QLT.

Plastic cover   Designed Paper Insert

Watch case

Designed paper circle is sandwiched between plastic cover and watch case. (Plastic circle snaps into case)

Pendant

Keychains

Buttons

Plates

APPENDIX

Resources

The resources listed are a sampling of the many vendors who provide supplies, information or equipment in the T-shirt industry.

THERMAL TRANSFER SHEETS (Primary Suppliers)

Laser Printer
Thermal Transfer Sheets

RAMCO Computer Supplies
455 Grove
Manteno, IL 60950
1-815-480-8081

Double Exposure
69 Main Street
Vincentown, NJ 08088
1-800-526-2822

QLT
95 Morton Street
New York, NY 10014
1-800-221-9832

Dot Matrix
Thermal Transfer Sheets

Double Exposure
69 Main Street
Vincentown, NJ 08088
1-800-526-2822

Wyndstone
1400 E. Touny Ave
DesPlaines, IL 60618
1-708-297-2330

Foto-Wear
101 Pocono Drive
Milford, PA 18337
1-717-296-4709

Dye-Sublimation
Thermal Transfer Sheets

Double Exposure
69 Main Street
Vincentown, NJ 08088
1-800-526-2822

Wyndstone
1400 E. Touny Ave
DesPlaines, IL 60618
1-708-297-2330

Foto-Wear
101 Pocono Drive
Milford, PA 18337
1-717-296-4709

Wax Thermal
Thermal Transfer Sheets

Double Exposure
69 Main Street
Vincentown, NJ 08088
1-800-526-2822

Wyndstone
1400 E. Touny Ave
DesPlaines, IL 60618
1-708-297-2330

Foto-Wear
101 Pocono Drive
Milford, PA 18337
1-717-296-4709

Ink Jet
Thermal Transfer Sheets

Double Exposure
69 Main Street
Vincentown, NJ 08088
1-800-526-2822

Wyndstone
1400 E. Touny Ave
DesPlaines, IL 60618
1-708-297-2330

Foto-Wear
101 Pocono Drive
Milford, PA 18337
1-717-296-4709

PhotoCopier
Thermal Transfer Sheets

Double Exposure
69 Main Street
Vincentown, NJ 08088
1-800-526-2822

Wyndstone
1400 E. Touny Ave
DesPlaines, IL 60618
1-708-297-2330

Foto-Wear
101 Pocono Drive
Milford, PA 18337
1-717-296-4709

866-783-4700
847-783-4700
www.fotowear.com

Thermal Transfer Sheets

Double Exposure
69 Main Street
Vincentown, NJ 08088
1-800-526-2822

Wyndstone
1400 E. Touny Ave
DesPlaines, IL 60618
1-708-297-2330

Foto-Wear
101 Pocono Drive
Milford, PA 18337
1-717-296-4709

RAMCO Computer Supplies
455 Grove
Manteno, IL 60950
1-815-480-8081

QLT
95 Morton Street
New York, NY 10014
1-800-221-9832

Air Waves
6567 Huntley Rd.
Columbus, OH 43229
1-800-468-7335

Thermal Printer Ribbons

RAMCO Computer Supplies
455 Grove
Manteno, IL 60950
1-815-480-8081

QLT
95 Morton Street
New York, NY 10014
1-800-221-9832

Thermal Laser Toner Cartridges (Dye-Sublimation Cartridges)

Black Lightening
Riddle Pond Road
West Topsham, VT 05086
1-800-252-2599

RAMCO Computer Supplies
455 Grove
Manteno, IL 60950
1-815-480-8081

QLT
95 Morton Street
New York, NY 10014
1-800-221-9832

Opaque Transfers
(print on dark fabric)
Wyndstone
1400 E. Touny Ave
DesPlaines, IL 60618
1-708-297-2330

Instant T's
121 Cannon Point Rd
Milledgeville, GA 31061
1-800-221-6186

Draw and wear

Double Exposure
69 Main Street
Vincentown, NJ 08088
1-800-526-2822

Foto-Wear
101 Pocono Drive
Milford, PA 18337
1-717-296-4709

RAMCO Computer Supplies
455 Grove
Manteno, IL 60950
1-815-480-8081

T-shirts (Blanks)

Amtex, Inc
2331 W. St. Paul Ave.
Chicago, Il 60647
1-800-421-Tees

Tees in Time
10722 Hanna Street
Beltsville, MD 20705
1-800-423-9282

Virginia Tees
Petersburg, VA
1-800-289-8099

Keystone Tees
1200 Roosevelt St
Reading, PA 19606
1-800-554-4869

H.L. Miller
536 Garfield Ave
Schuylkill Haven, PA 17972

Hanes Printables has a large group of North American distrubutors. Use their Product Locator line, 1-800-685-7557 to locate the dealer nearest you.

Heat/Hat Press

Hix
1201 E 27th St
Pittsburg, KS 66762
1-800-835-0606

Insta Graphic Systems
13925 E 166th St, Box 7900
Cerritos, CA 90702
1-800-421-6971

Able Transfer Presses
16004 Broadway Ave #207
Maple Heights, OH44137
1-800-600-6267

BOO-Z Wearhouse
4972 Louisville Rd
Salvisda, KY 40372
1-800-552-4439

Stahl's
20600 Stephans Drive
St.Clair Shores, MI 48080
1-800-521-9702

Color Printers:
Fargo Electronics
7901 Flying Cloud Dr
Eden Prarie MN 55344
1-800-327-4622

Photo CD Imaging (by mail)
LASERQUICK Imaging
27375 S.W. Parkway Ave
Wilsonville, OR 97070
1-800-477-2679

Uniforms (Non-sports type)
Hyman's
P.O.Box 71171
N. Charleston, SC 29415
1-800-354-9626

Team Uniforms
Empire Sporting Goods
443 Broadway
New York, NY 10013
1-800-2213455

Arrowear Athletic Apparel
113 E. Merric Rd
Valley Stream, NY 11580
1-516-872-0606

Pressed-on Lettering
Sunbelt Lettering
P.O. Box 15302
Pensacola FL 32514
1-800-874-1024

Discount Transfer
10429 Plano Rd #102
Dallas, TX 75238
1-800-527-7060

Insta Graphic Systems
13925 E 166th St, Box 7900
Cerritos, CA 90702
1-800-421-6971

Impulse Wear
225 Business Center Drive
Blacklick, OH 43004
1-800- 255-1280

Stahl's
20600 Stephans Drive
St.Clair Shores, MI 48080
1-800-521-9702

Software by Mail
PC/MAC Warehouse
P.O.Box 3013
1720 Oak Street
Lakewood, NJ 08701
1-800-255-6227

PC/MAC Zone
17411 NE Union Hill Rd
Building A Suite140
Redmond, WA 98052
1-800-24809948

PC/MAC Connection
6 Mill Street
Marlow, NH 03456
1-800-800-5555

T-Shirt Transfer Systems
Eagle Graphic Equipment
7704 19th Avenue Drive West
Bradenton, FL 34209
1-800-523-7005

CompuGrafix
13951 Scottsdale Rd
Scottsdale, AZ 85254
1-800-678-175

X-PRESS
111 Cloverleaf Drive
Winston Salem, NC 27103
1-800-334-0425

RPL Supplies, Inc.
280 Midland Avenue
Saddle Brook, NJ 07662
1-800-524-0914

Color Separations
Serichrome
4841 Gretna Street
Dallas, TX 75207
1-214-631-5400

Private Labels
Bach Label Co
1212 S. San Pedro St
Los Angeles, CA 090015-2665

Express Mark
505 Cuthbertson Street
Monroe, NC 28110
1-800-322-1746

Tye-Dye
Grateful Dye
2139 S. Sheraton Blvd
Denver, CO 80227
1-303-763-9730

Bandanas/Handkerchiefs
Marks Handkerchief Mfg
P.O.Box 2226
Augusta, GA 30913-2226
1-800-388-2579

Aprons

The Apron Works
1413 East 20th Street
Los Angeles, Ca 90011
1-800-344-7884

Aprons, Etc.
53 Donkle Road
Greenville, SC 29609
1-800-467-1996

Caps

Capco
252 Beinoris Drive
Wood Dale, IL 60191
1-800-833-5856

Madhatter
1228 E. Fairground Street
Marion, OH 43302
1-800-521-2353

Infant Blanks/Bibs

Comco Inc
P.O.Box 9039
North Saint Paul, MN 55109
1-800-328-9658

Embroidery Equipment

Meistergram
3517 W. Wendover Ave
Greensboro, NC 27407
1-800-321-0486

Bibs

Cape Cod Textine
338 Route 130
Sandwich, MA 02563
1-800-543-4075

QLT
95 Morton Street
New York, NY 10014
1-800-221-9832

Pet Apparel

Allegre Fashions
7370 W 20th Street
Hialeah, FL33016
1-800-835-6487

Irregular/Seconds

Malones
1514 Jake Alexander Blvd,W
Salisbury, NC 28144
1-704-633-4854

RPM Textiles
14946 Court St
Moulton, AL 35650
1-205-974-0480

Ties/Suspenders

Daitch & Compan
1216 Broad St. POBox 699
Augusta, GA 30903

Umbrellas

Toppers
1450 Grandview Ave
Thorofare, NJ 08086
1-800-523-0825

Kites/Windsocks

Source Master
86 Gibson Road #6
Templeton, CA 93465

Key Rings

RPL Supplies, Inc.
280 Midland Avenue
Saddle Brook, NJ 07662
1-800-524-0914

Chairs

Academy Awards
3720 South Irby St
Florence, SC 29505
1-800-972-0715

Bumper Stickers

Graphic Supply
1131 S. 77th E .Ave
Tulsa, OK74112
1-800-234-0765

Blank Car Shades

Classic Car Shades
7238 N.W. 70 Street
Miami, FL 33160
1-800- 487-4233

Stadium Cushions

All American Mfg.
Rt 2, Box AA
Boyceville, WI
1-800-643-2222

Wallets

Source Master
86 Gibson Road #6
Templeton, CA 93465
1-800-272-2910

Flags

Eder Flag Mfg. Co.
1000W. Rawson Ave.
Oak Creek, WI 531721487
1-800-558-6044

Metal Printing

Novachrome
3345 Vincent Road
Pleasant Hill, CA 94523
1-800-788-6682

QLT
95 Morton Street
New York, NY 10014
1-800-221-9832

Belt Printing

Universal Sportswear
1-800-444-6484

Software
Broderbund
P.O.Box 6125
Novato, CA 94948-6125

Adobe Systems
1585 Charleston Road
Montain View, CA 94039

Aldus
411 First Avenue South
Seatle WA 9804-2871
1-206-622-5500

Corel Draw
1600 Carling Ave
Ottawa
Ontario
CanadaK1Z1R7
1-613-728-3733

Clip Art
Images With Impact
114 Second Ave, South
Edmonds, WA 98020

Image Club
10545 W. Donges Court
Milwaukee, WI 53224
1-800-662-9410

T/Maker
1390 Villa Street
Mountain View, CA 94041
1-415-962-0195

Dover Clip-Art (books)
31 E 2nd St
Mineola, N.Y. 11501

Tote Bags/Bags
Toppers
318 S. Blackhorse Pike
Blackwood, NJ 08012
1-800-523-0825

The Bag Connection
2500-B Hoover Ave
National City, CA 91950
1-800-730-BAGS
QLT
95 Morton Street
New York, NY 10014
1-800-221-9832

Large Size T-Shirts:
Just Big (Sizes up to 8XL)
1-704-391-3000

Rub-off Sheets:
Lettraset
40 Eisenhower Drive
Paramuse, NJ 07652
1-800-343-8973

Dolls
QLT
95 Morton Street
6th Floor
New York, NY 10014
1-800-221-9832

Instant T's
121 Cannon Point Rd
Milledgeville, GA 31061
1-800-221-6186

Canon Laser Copier Locations
Canon USA
1-800-652-2666

Licensed Sporting Products
Bodek and Rhodes
2951 Grant Ave
Philadelphia, PA 19114
1-800-523-2721

Copyright
Copyright Office
Library of Congress
Room 401
Washington, DC 20540
1-202-287-6840

Screenprinting Equipment
Antec
POBox 3787
Charlottesville, VA 2903
1-800-552-6832

CATCO
12201 Northwest 35th St
Coral Springs, FL 33065
1-800-869-6338

CD Rom Drives
NEC
1255 Michael Dr
Woodale, IL 60191
1-708-860-9500

CD Clip Art/Stock Photos
Educorp
7434 Trade Street
San Diego, CA 92121
1-800-843-9497

Mouse Pads
Mous Trak
2701 Conestoga Dr #123
Carson City, NV 89706

Black Lightening
Riddle Pond Road
West Topsham, VT 05086
1-800-252-2599

Kodak CD Vendors
1-800-242-2424

Heat Press Locations
Kinko
800-743-COPY

Staples Office Supplies
617-229-0369

Insta Graphic Systems
1-800-421-6971

Mug Presses and Supplies
QLT
95 Morton Street
6th Floor
New York, NY 10014
1-800-221-9832

X-PRESS
111 Cloverleaf Drive
Winston Salem, NC 27103
1-800-334-0425

RPL Supplies, Inc.
280 Midland Avenue
Saddle Brook, NJ 07662
1-800-524-0914

The Color Factory
9200 Tropico Dr
La Mesa, CA 91941
1-800-669-0830

Instant T's
121 Cannon Point Rd
Milledgeville, GA 31061
1-800-221-6186

Cactus Coatings
1031 S. 15th St
Grand Junction, CO 81501
1-800-440-6847

Trade Magazines-
Flash Magazine
Riddle Pond Road
West Topsham, Vt 05086
1-800-252-2599
*(If you use a laser printer,
you can't live without this pub!)*

Printwear
P.O.Box 1416
Broomfield, CO 80038
1-303-469-0424

Imprintables Today
1-602-990-1101

ScreenPlay
407 Gilbert Ave
Cincinnati, OH 45202
1-513-421-2050

Impressions
13760 Noel Road, Suite 500
Dallas, TX 75240
1-800-527-0207

Associations/Institutes:
Screenprinter Assn
10015 Main St
Fairfax, VA 22031
1-703-385-1335

U.S.Screenprinting Institute
7419 E. Helen Drive
Scottsdale, AZ 85260
1-800-624-6532

Related Books:
*Make at Least $100,000 This
Year With A Heat Transfer Press*
Lancaster Publishing Group
P.O.Box 404
Lancaster, KY 40444

How to Print T-Shirts (screenprint)
Union Inc
453 Broad Ave
Ridgefield, NJ 07657
1-800-526-0455

Great T-Shirt Graphics
ST Publications
407 Gilbert Ave
Cincinnati, OH 45202
1-800-925-1110

GLOSSARY
OF
TERMS

Belt Printing - An ink based printing process that prints a graphic on the entire surface of the garment.

Digitizing - Translating a photo's various shades of black or color into numbers (*digits*) which a computer can read and manipulate.

Dot Matrix - A type of printer which presses a series of pins through a ribbon, onto paper which creates dots. The dots are placed close together in such a way as to create letters and numbers.

Dye-Sublimation - A type of full-color printer which melts dye from a ribbon, transferring it onto paper.

Emulsion Down - Printing a mirrored image of the graphic on a computer screen. The image is again reversed when heat pressed onto a surface, such as fabric.

Hat Press - Similar to the Heat Press but equipped with a convex heated and stationary surface that facilitates heat pressing the curved front of caps.

Heart Patch - A three to four inch printed impression on a shirt at the approximate position of the wearer's heart.

Heat Press - A piece of equipment having a hinged heated surface which is pressed against a stationary surface. It is used to press heat transfers and pressed-on letters onto various garments.

Ink-Jet - A type of printer which sprays a carefully controlled ink dye onto the surface of paper. Some ink jet printers are capable of full color printing.

Litho - A conventional printing process used to produce large volumes of transfer sheets

Pressed-on Lettering - Various types of fabrics cut into letter or number shapes which are glued onto a garment.

Rub-off Sheet - Lettering which is rubbed off of a sheet of clear plastic onto paper. These sheets contain the entire alphabet and numbers in one typeface.

Screen Printing - A printing process which forces ink through a screen onto a surface such as a fabric.

Thermal - A heat process used in color printers that melts wax or dye, transferring it onto paper. The same heat process melts the coating on heat transfer sheets onto another surface such as fabric.

Thermal Wax - A type of full-color printer which melts wax from a ribbon, transferring it onto paper.

Tiling - Several sheets of paper on which a small part of a design is printed. These sheets are then put together to form the whole design.

Transfer Sheet - A specially coated sheet of paper which receive toner, dye or ink from a printer ribbon or cartridge.

Tye Dye - A method of creating a random design on a garment using fabric dyes and tying the garment in various configurations.

Index